4-23-18

D1611821

here is new york

here is new york

a democracy of photographs

conceived and organized by

alice rose george – gilles peress – michael shulan – charles traub

Park City Public Library
2107 E. 61st St. N.
Park City, KS 67219-1904

Scalo Zurich – Berlin – New York

www.hereisnewyork.org

here is new york, an exhibition and sale of photographs of the World Trade Center tragedy that four of us organized about a week after 9/11, began on the ground floor of a small four-story building that I own with two others at 116 Prince Street in SoHo, some fifteen blocks north of Ground Zero. The space, which for twenty years was a women's clothing shop, had been vacant since that August. On September 11th I was sitting at my laptop in the back when the first plane roared over the building. The idea for the exhibition was sparked by an Ancient Greek poem about despair that I saw written out in magic marker on a sheet of newspaper and stuck up on a wall the following afternoon. By this time the police had closed off the neighborhood and people were wandering about aimlessly in surgical masks. I went back to my loft and dug out a nondescript photograph of the Trade Center which I had acquired sometime earlier at the flea market, and taped it up in the window of the empty shop.

A day or two later, Gilles Peress, who had been down at Ground Zero photographing for the *New Yorker*, called me on my cell phone and asked what I was doing. I replied that I was in the shop staring at a group of people staring at a photograph, and was thinking about putting up some more. "Do it," he said, simply. We met the following evening with two other friends and colleagues, Alice Rose George and Charles Traub, and quickly devised a plan. In those turbulent days it seemed as if everyone in New York had a camera, and we decided that the exhibition should be as broad and inclusive as possible, open to "anybody and everybody": not just photojournalists and other professional photographers, but bankers, rescue workers, artists and children—amateurs of every stripe.

The key, we knew, was to act fast. Alice, a photo editor and independent curator, began calling magazines and newspapers and every photographer she knew, asking them to spread the word and send pictures. Gilles suggested that we scan every submission to turn them into digital files and print them with inkjet printers. Charles, a photographer and Chairman of the MFA Department of Photography and the Related Media at New York's School of Visual Arts, set about rounding up equipment and student volunteers. I visited several galleries with Alice, looking for some appropriate way to hang the pictures, ultimately—inspired by a snapshot I had taken the previous spring of great clouds of laundry suspended from wires above a tiny street in Naples, Italy—finding it in the local hardware store. Since we had decided to sell the prints for $25 each to raise money for the children of victims, I also looked for a charitable organization through which the money could be distributed. We settled on the Children's Aid Society, which had already set up a fund for the children of restaurant workers, illegal immigrants, and others who were not likely to be provided for by other sources. We are very honored to be associated with them.

The exhibition opened on September 25, and by the beginning of its second week there was a long line at the door. We had originally intended to close on October 15, but by then we had been absolutely inundated with pictures, had filled the original storefront, and had expanded to another which also was vacant, in the building next door. Over the course of the next month we announced two more closings, but eventually we decided to stay open until Christmas. By December 24 we had sold more than thirty thousand prints, had constructed a website, had sent a number of exhibitions on the road, and had made commitments to do several others. On January 2, when a crowd began to collect in the street, we realized that we had no choice but to reopen.

here is new york is a very small part of the story of 9/11, but in its own way it became a microcosm of what took place in the disaster's aftermath at Ground Zero and elsewhere in the city. Not an art exhibition in the conventional sense—partly an impromptu memorial, partly a rescue effort, and partly a testimonial of support for those who were actually doing the rescuing—it became a rallying point for the neighborhood and for the community at large. Thousands of photographers selflessly donated pictures; hundreds of thousands of people came to view and to buy them at Prince Street and at our other exhibitions; literally millions of people have looked at them on our website. None of this would have been possible without the hundreds of highly skilled and dedicated volunteers who have been with *here is new york* since its inception, not a few of whom have continually worked ten- and twelve-hour days, six and seven days a week. Along with the photographers, they deserve most of the credit for *here is new york*'s existence. Alice, Gilles, Charles, and I knew from the outset that the exhibition would be powerful, but not for a moment did we think that lines would stretch around the block, disrupting traffic and local businesses. Nor did we imagine that a steady stream of fire trucks and police cars would draw up in front of the building at all hours, the crews who were piling into the storefronts to look at the pictures trailing that horrific smell of Ground Zero that everyone in Lower Manhattan came to know only too well. We started with the help of some friends and a devoted cadre of Charles's students, but their ranks quickly swelled with photographers, neighbors, artists, housewives, and lawyers—again, "anybody and everybody". They read about the exhibition in the newspaper, saw a report about it on TV, or came to Prince Street to submit pictures. Then they took it upon themselves to scan pictures, color-correct pictures, print pictures, label pictures, hang pictures, sell pictures, ship pictures, and database pictures, as well as to build our website, network our computers, arrange our exhibitions, program our slide shows, do our contracts and tax filings, work on the production of this book, and do everything else that *here is new york*, by whatever logic, has come to do. We are indebted to them beyond measure. Out of something truly unspeakable has come something truly wonderful: love.

Photography was the perfect medium to express what happened on 9/11, since it is democratic by its very nature and infinitely reproducible. The tragedy at Ground Zero struck all New Yorkers equally, leaving none of us immune to shock or grief. Although the disaster was the lead story in every newspaper in the world, and searing footage of the planes destroying the towers was running on television twenty-four hours a day, to New Yorkers this wasn't a news story: it was an unabsorbable nightmare. In order to come to grips with all of the imagery that was haunting us, it was essential, we thought, to reclaim it from the media and stare at it without flinching. Terrorism was all too familiar in other parts of the world, but it had rarely happened in the United States, and never on such a scale. Besides announcing that this is the face of our city's tragedy, the title *here is new york* declares that we understand the problem of terrorism to be a global one that respects no geographic or cultural boundaries. After 9/11, New York is Everywhere.

This book contains nearly a thousand of the more than five thousand pictures that some three thousand photographers submitted to the exhibition. It has not been edited to showcase the "best" or the "strongest" images, but to give the most coherent sense of the whole. *here is new york* has by now amassed one of the largest photographic archives in world history devoted to a single event. But whereas after other events of this magnitude one striking picture has sometimes come to stand for, or to symbolize, what happened, the one picture which will probably come to stand for the World Trade Center tragedy will be *all* of these pictures. What was captured by these photographs—captured with every conceivable kind of apparatus, from Leicas and digital Nikons to homemade pinhole cameras and little plastic gizmos that schoolchildren wear on their wrists—is truly astonishing: not only grief, and shock, and courage, but a beauty that is at once infernal and profoundly uplifting. The pictures speak both to the horror of what happened on 9/11 (and is still happening),

and to the way it can and must be countered by us all. They speak not with one voice, but with one purpose, saying that to make sense of this terrifying new phase in our history we must break down the barriers that divide us.

The guiding principle of *here is new york* is simple: if one photograph tells *a* story, thousands of photographs not only tell thousands of stories but perhaps begin to tell *the* story if they are allowed to speak for themselves, to each other, and to the viewer directly—not framed either by glass, metal, or wood, or by preconception or editorial comment. In the political sphere it is this principle, after all, which America's Founding Fathers advanced when they developed the notion of democracy—that wisdom lies not in the vision and will of any one individual, or small group of individuals, but in the collective vision of us all.

As with print sales from our exhibitions, the net proceeds from the sale of this book will be donated to the Children's Aid Society and other worthy charities. We hope that it will stand as a living memorial to those who lost their lives on 9/11, as well as a tribute to those who came so valiantly to our aid. It is a testament to the courage and humanity of all New Yorkers. Every picture submitted to *here is new york* shows without question that terrorism can never succeed anywhere.

The entire archive of more than five thousand photographs can be viewed on our website: www.hereisnewyork.org. Seeing is not only believing. Seeing is *seeing*.

—Michael Shulan

"...The city, for the first time in its long history, is destructible. A single flight of planes no bigger than a wedge of geese can quickly end this island fantasy, burn the towers, crumble the bridges, turn the underground passages into lethal chambers, cremate the millions. The intimation of mortality is part of New York now: in the sound of jets overhead, in the black headlines of the latest edition."

—E.B. White, *Here is New York,* 1949

Park City Public Library
2107 E. 61st St. N.
Park City, KS 67219-1904

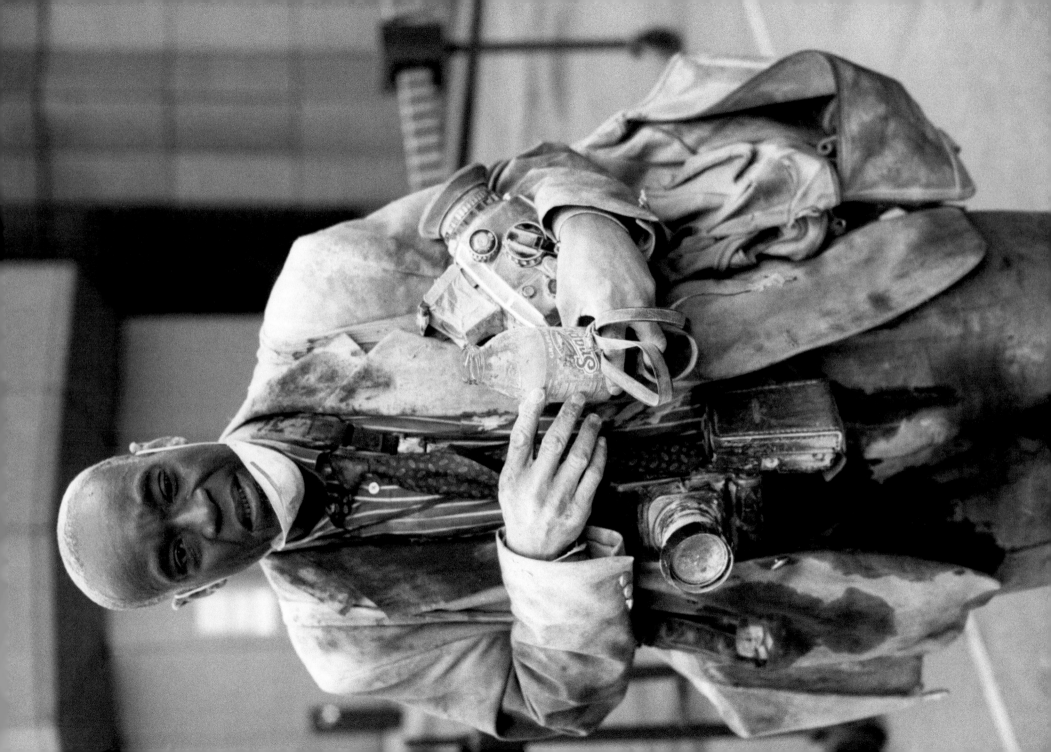

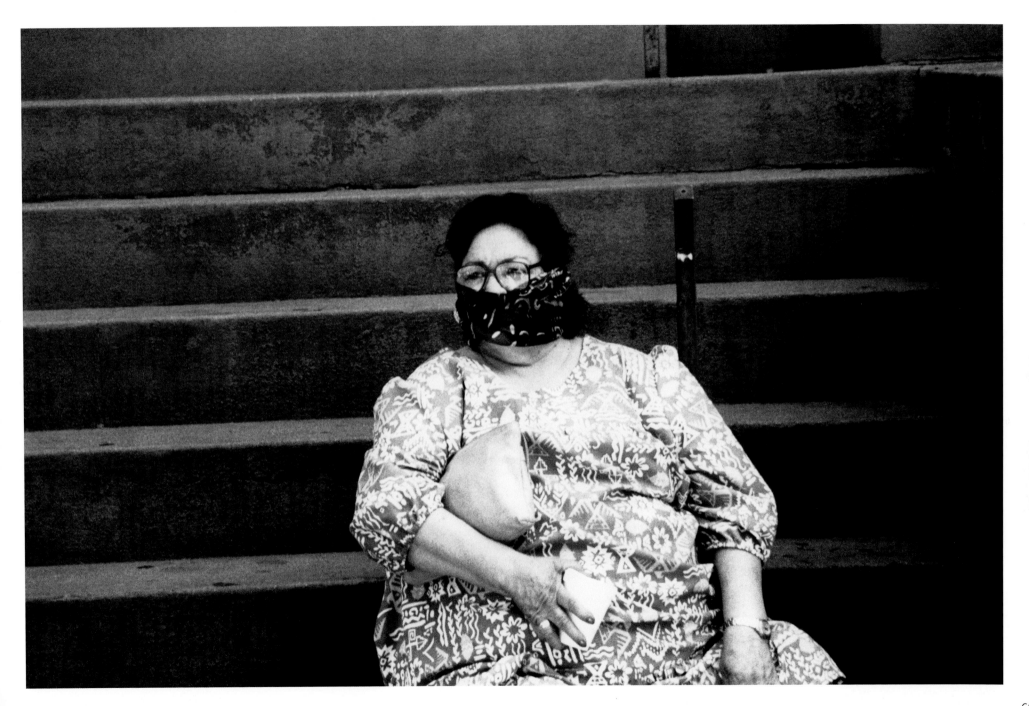

74

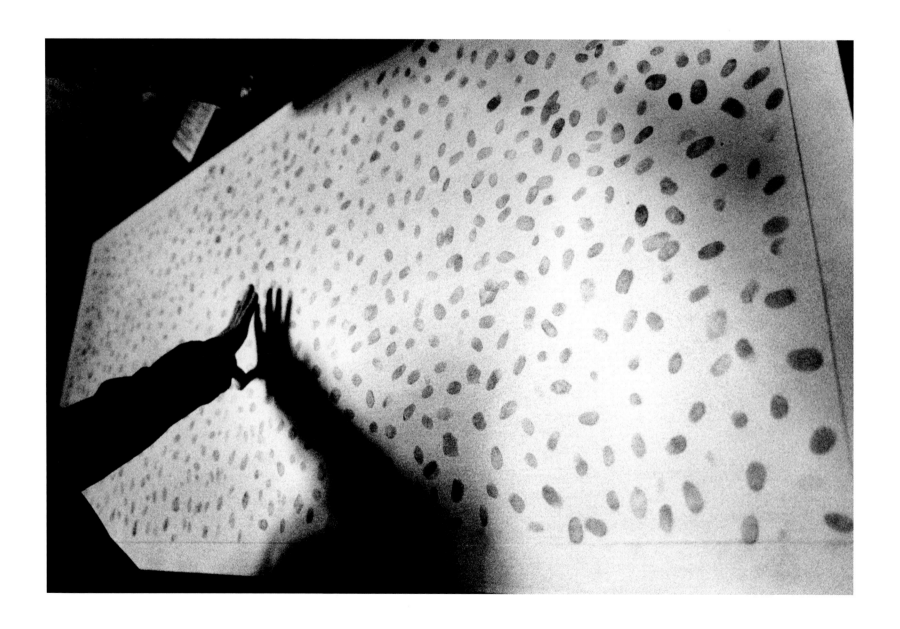

94

102

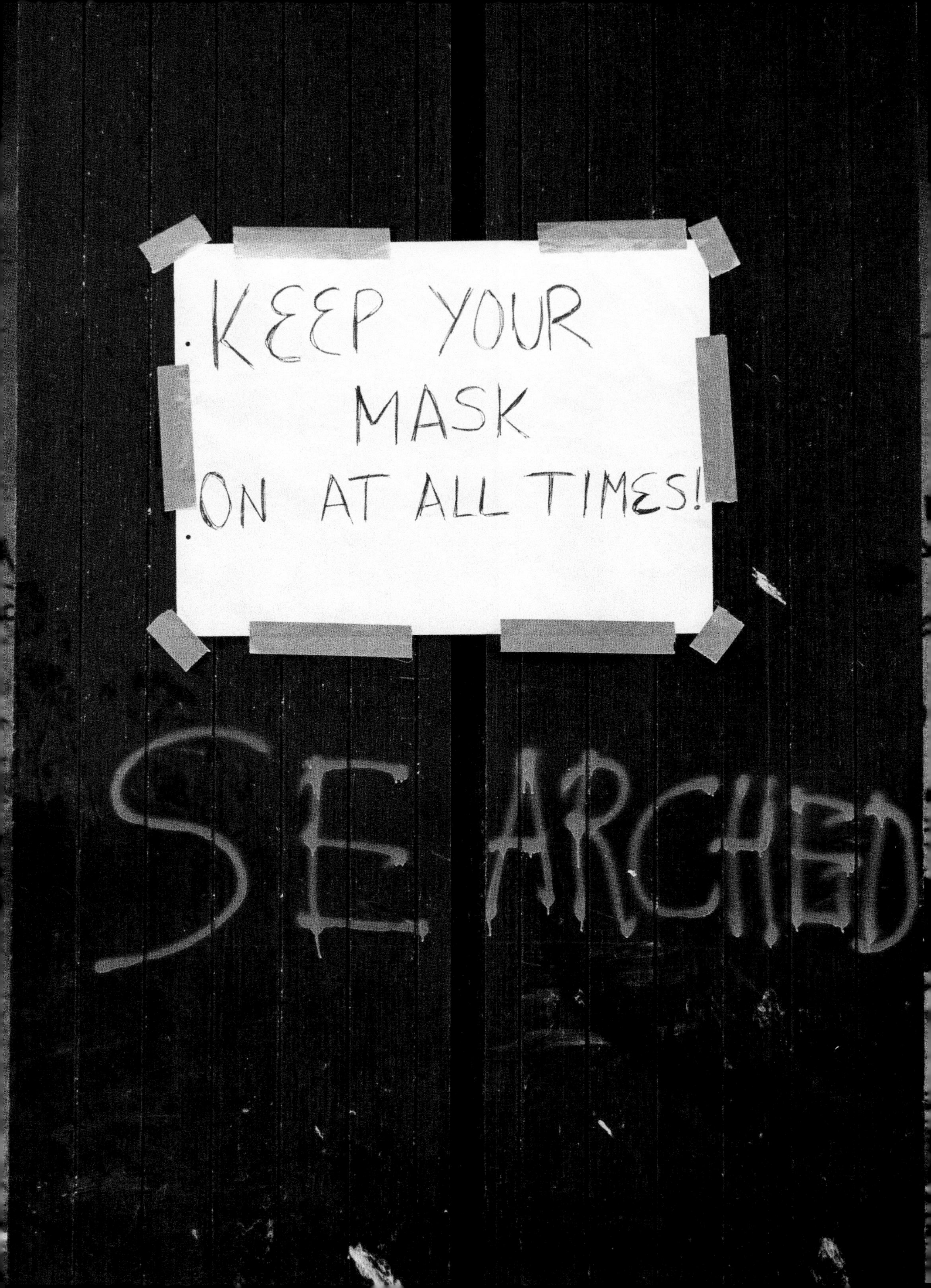
KEEP YOUR
MASK
ON AT ALL TIMES!
SEARCHED

111

113

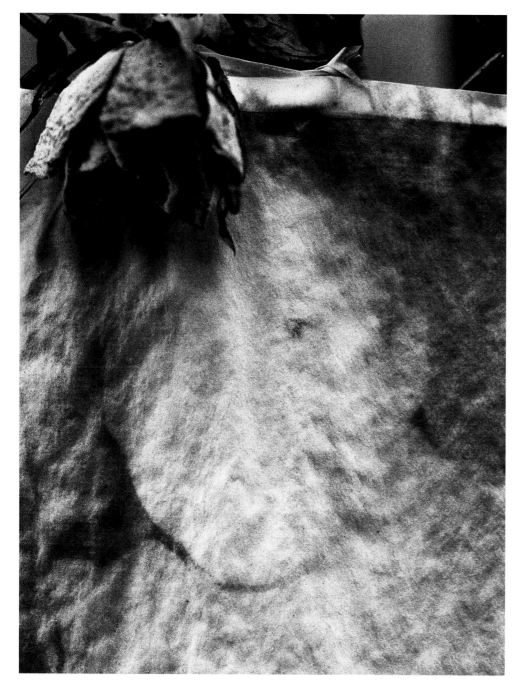

127

127

133

136

141

148

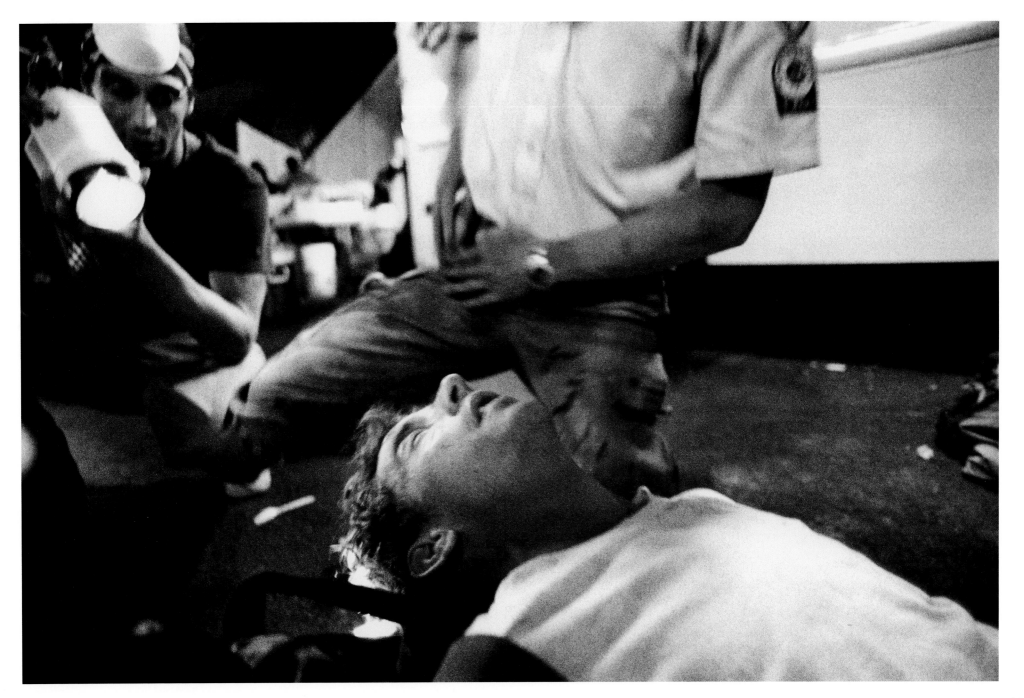

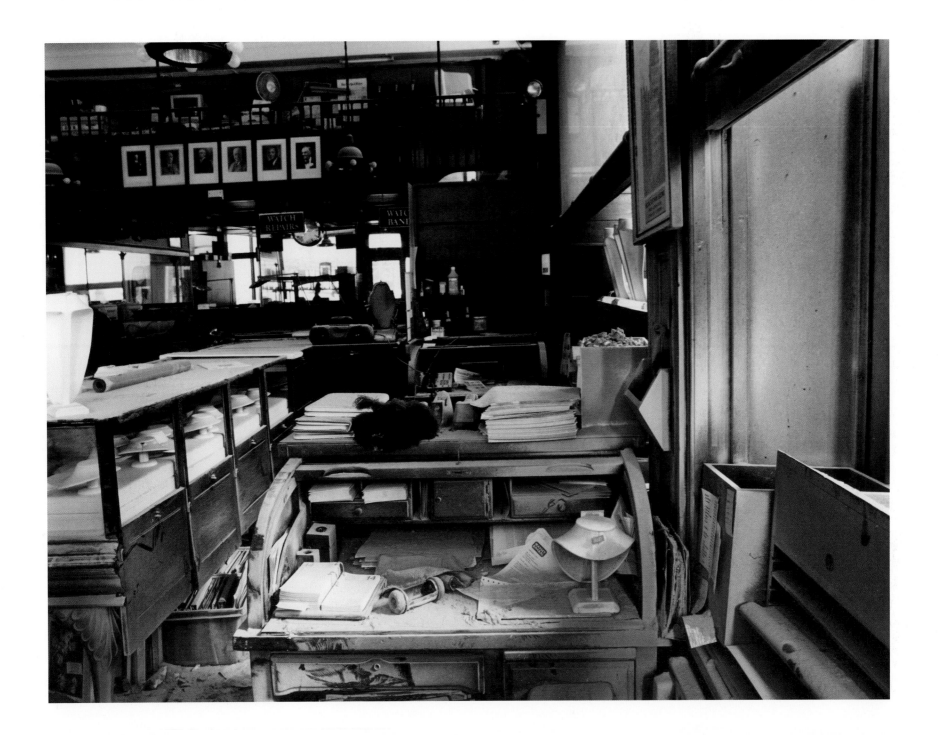

188

193

AM10:06
SEP 11 2001

DIRECTV.

Due to today's tragic events, this channel will not be seen today

Our thoughts go out to the victims and their families.

211

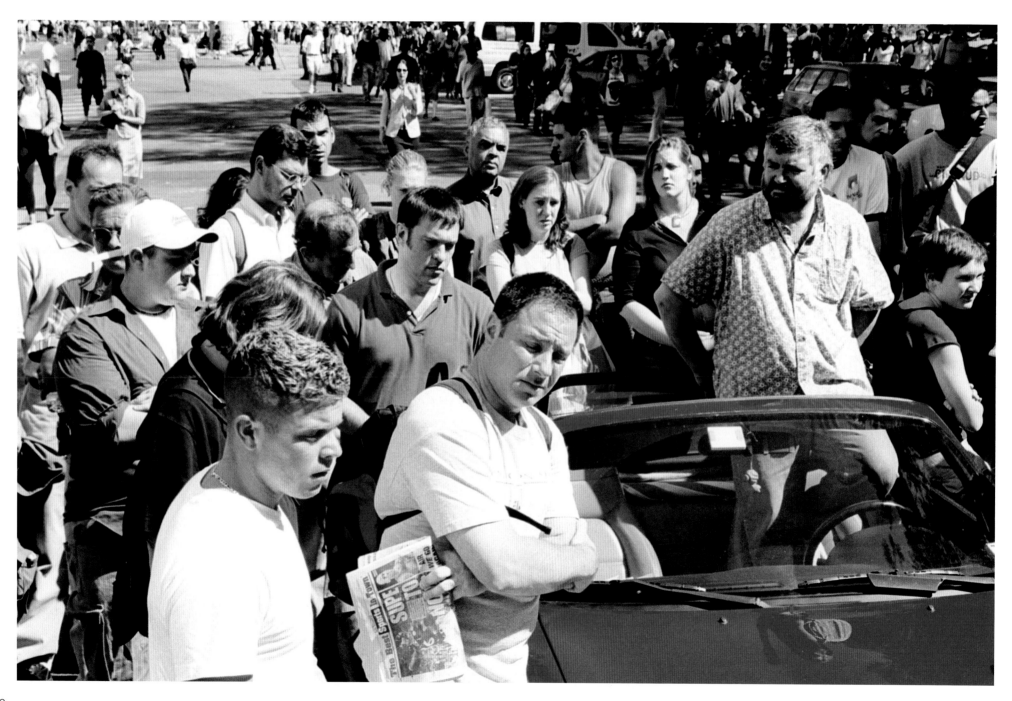

212

218

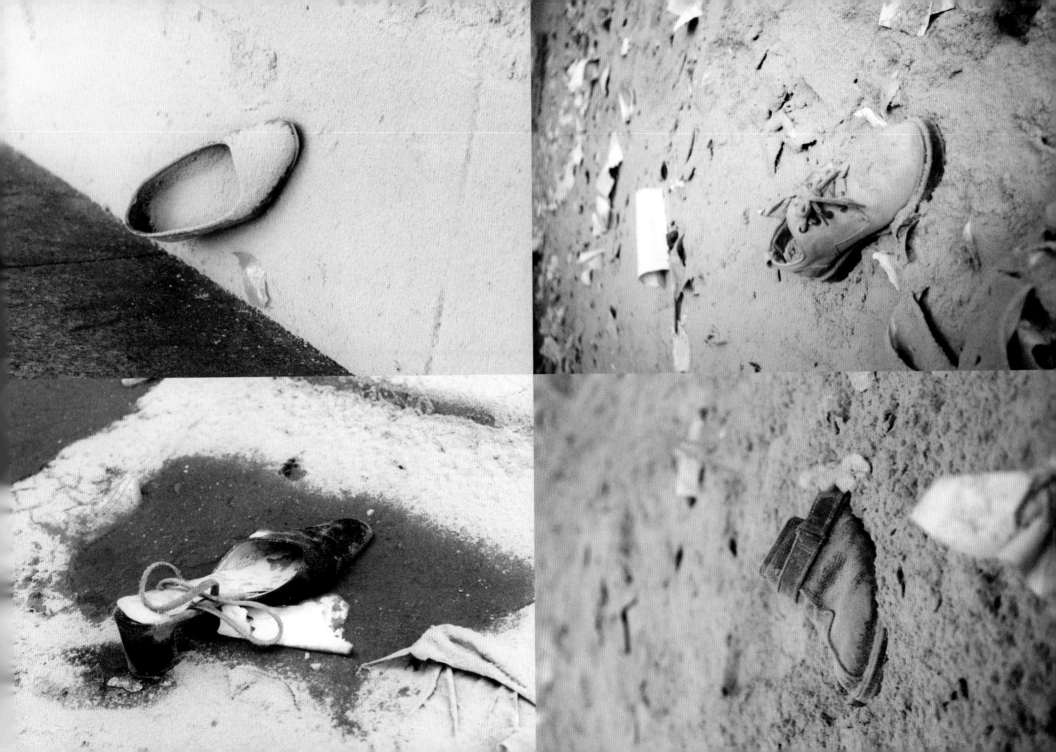

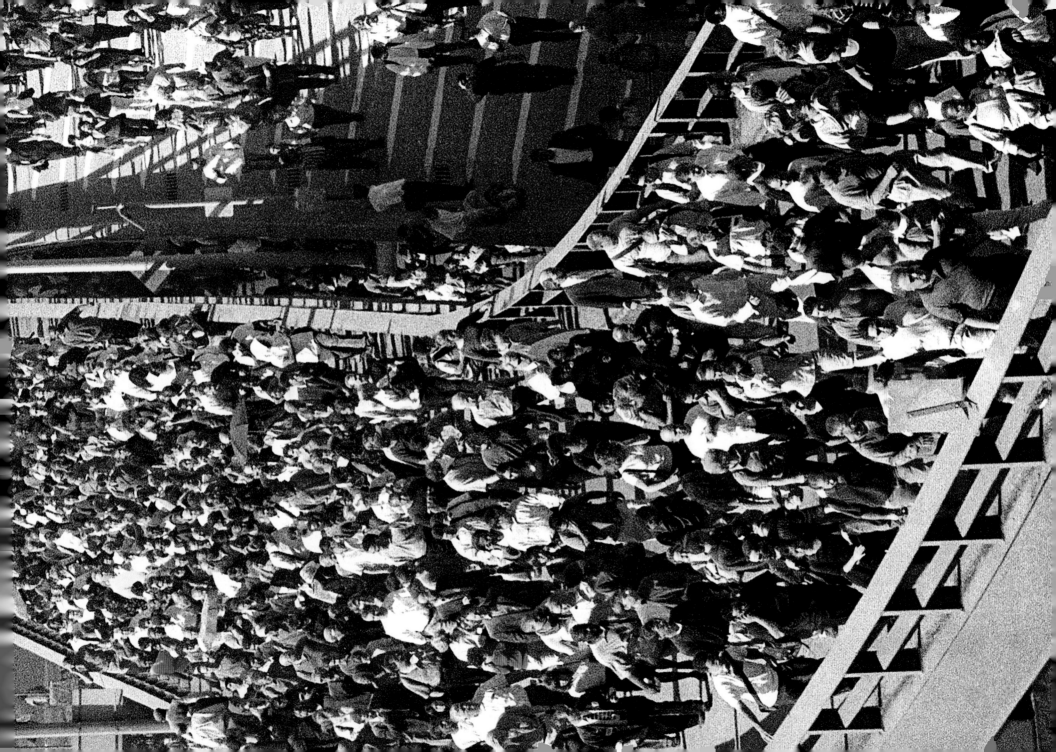

288

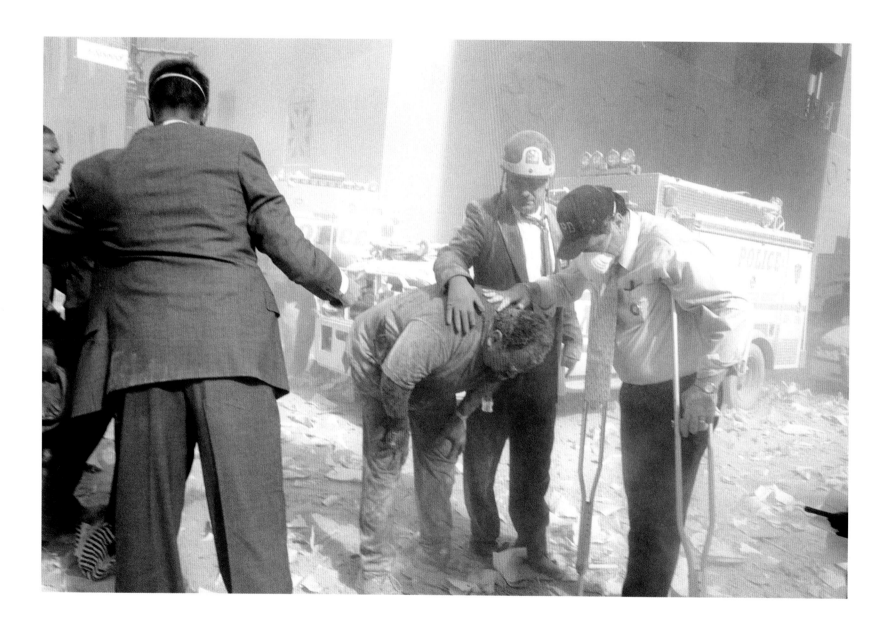

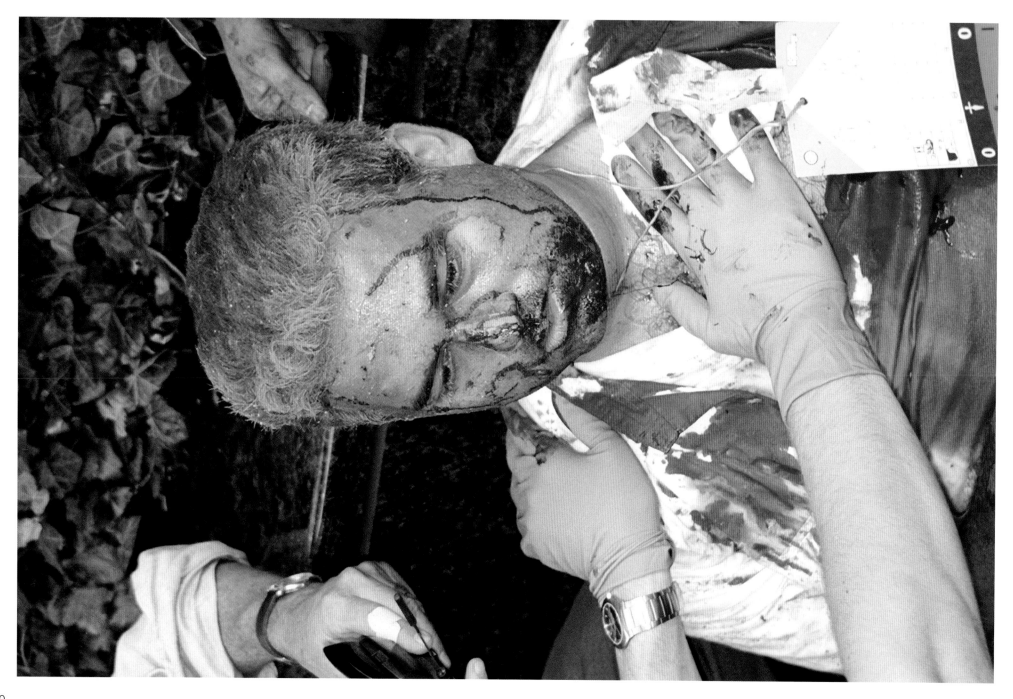

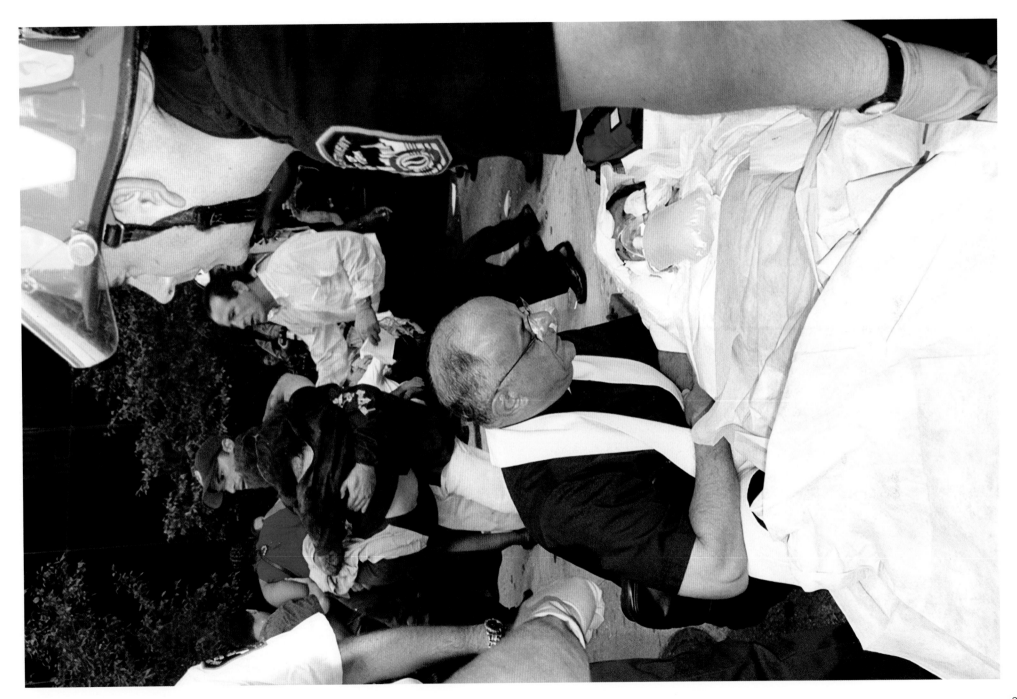

331

337

338

358

372

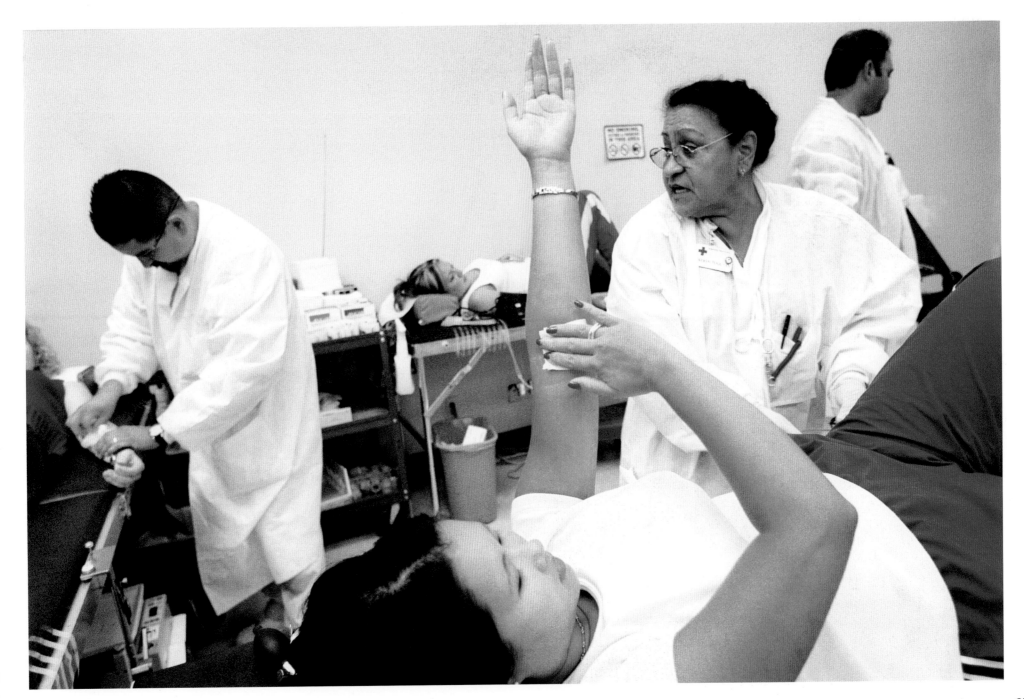

380

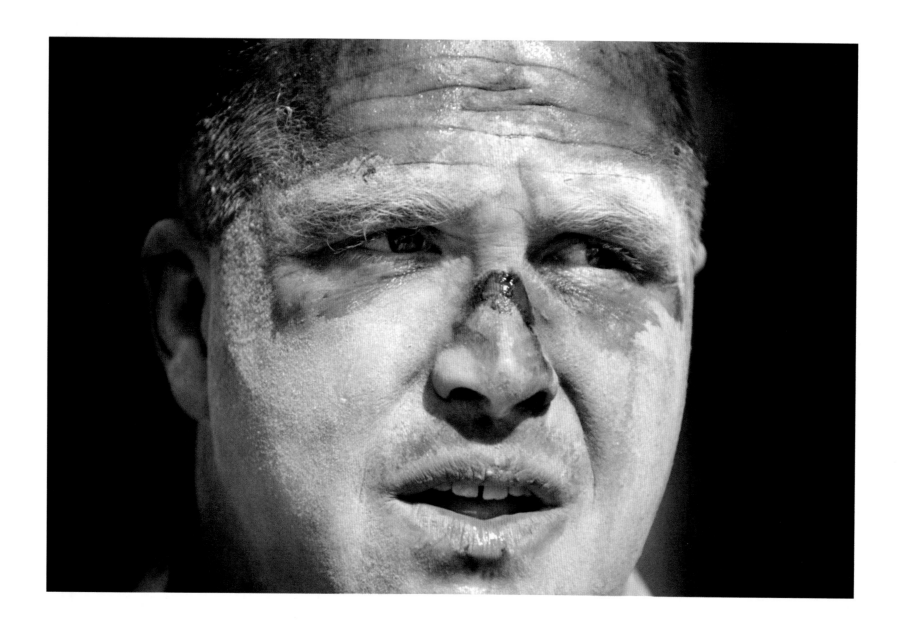

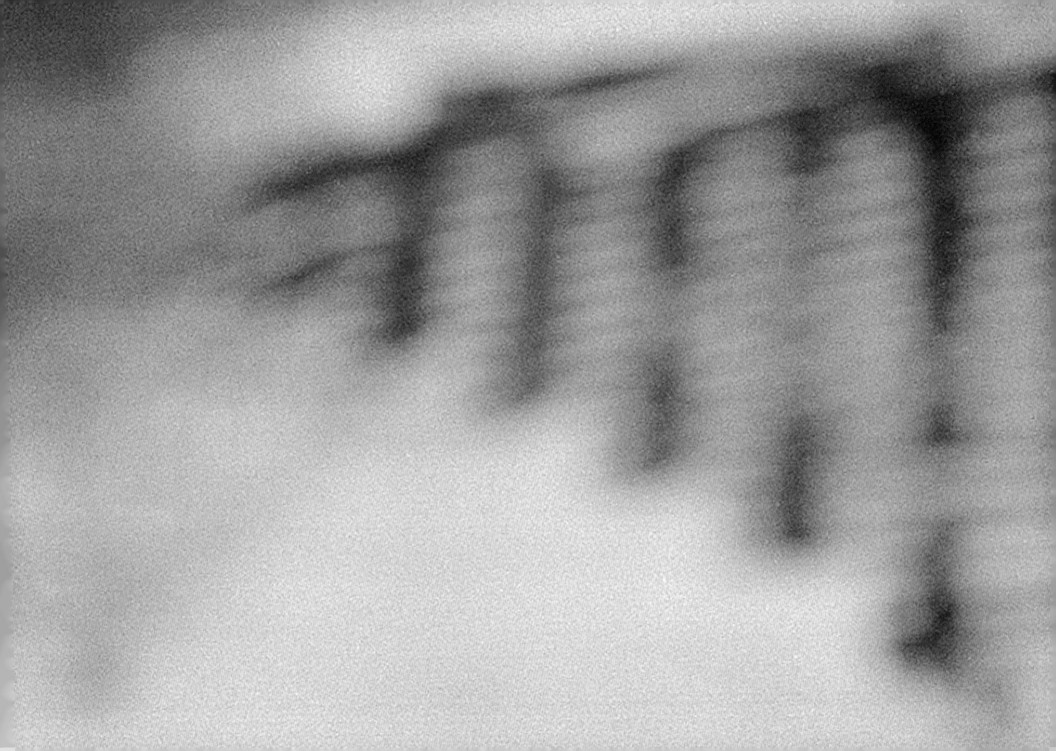

403

412

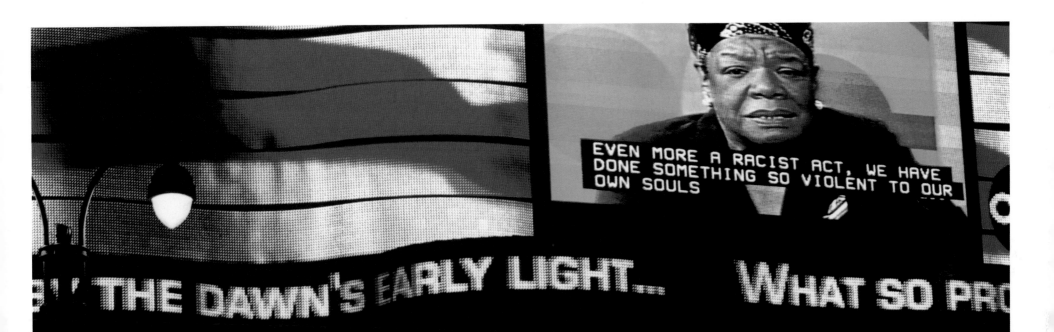

BREAKING NEWS
REPORTS: PART OF WORLD TRADE
CENTER TOWER COLLAPSES

CNN
LIVE

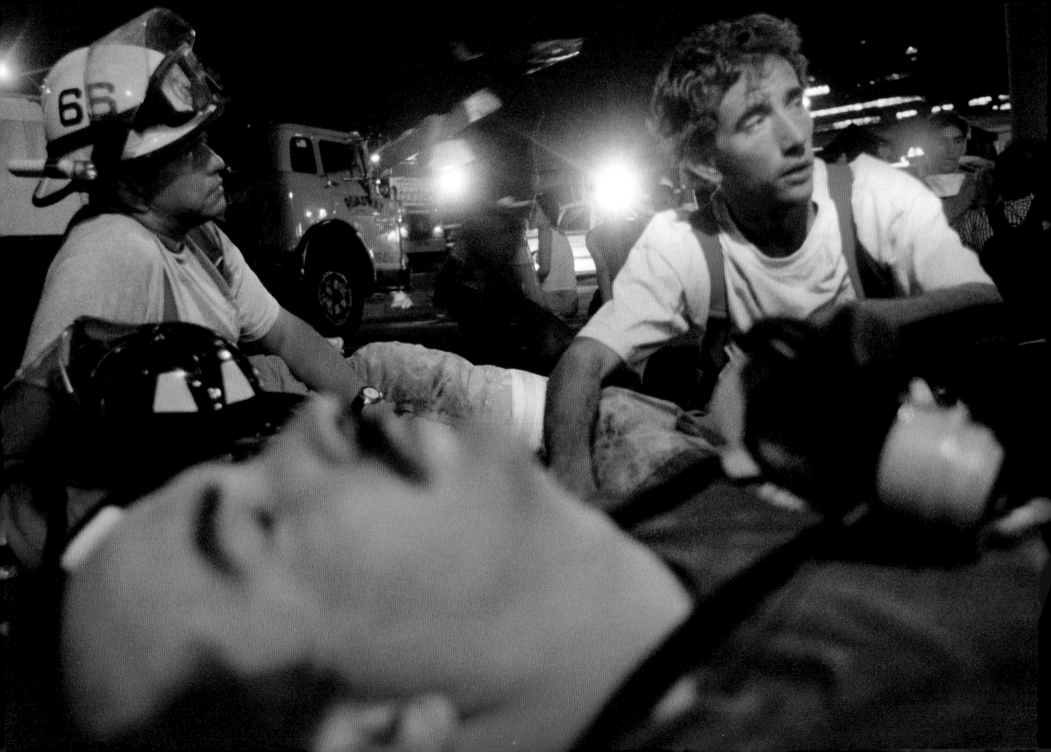

430

434

443

444

445

SALAAM·BOMBAY
INDIAN·CUISINE
WE·ARE·OPEN

CROSS

447

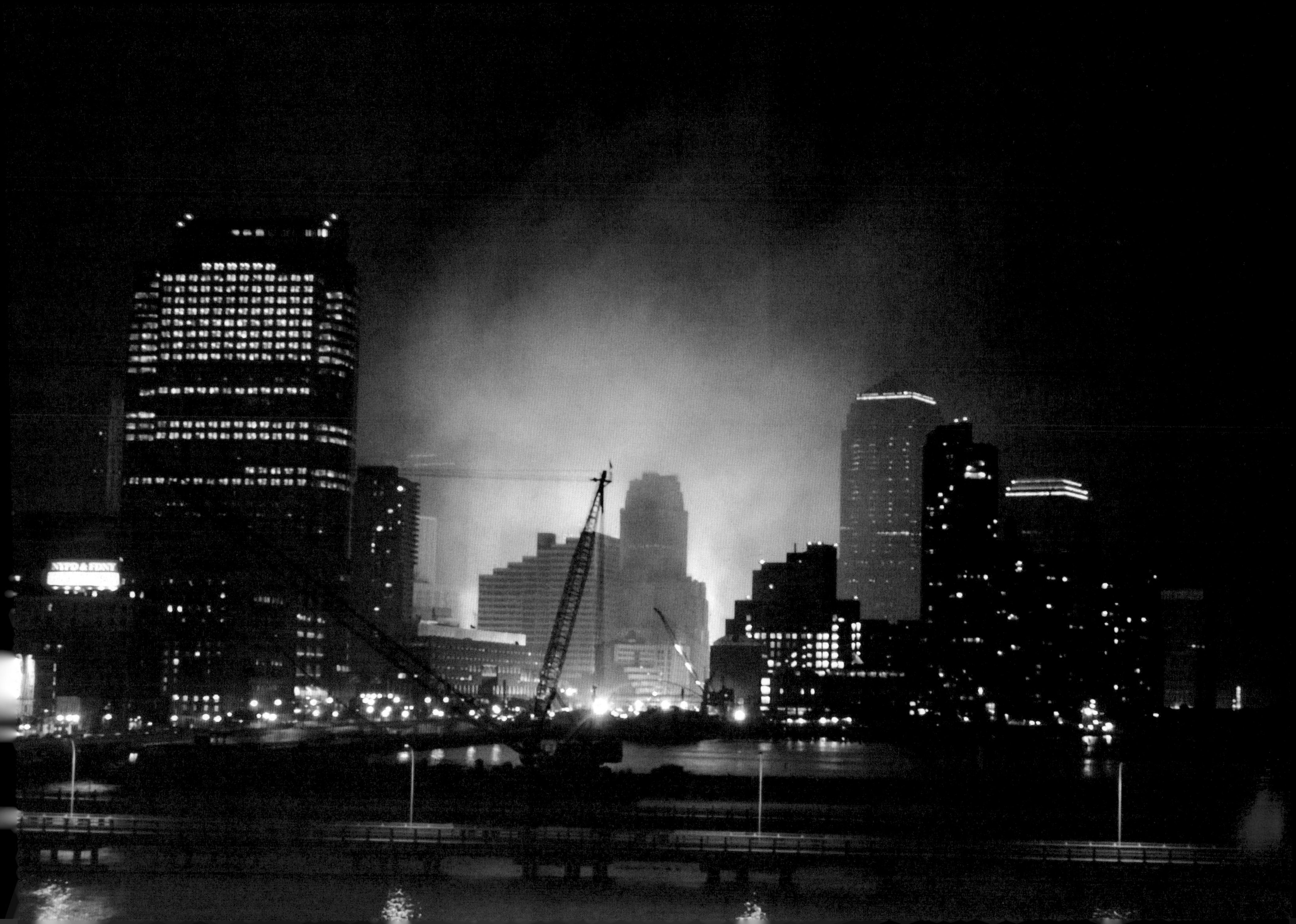

Monday, September 10, 2001 - 8:00 P.M.

Tuesday, September 11, 2001 - 8:00 P.M.

452

454

You are Alive.

ING PERSON:

EL ROSETTI

TC TOWER 2   105th FLOOR

494

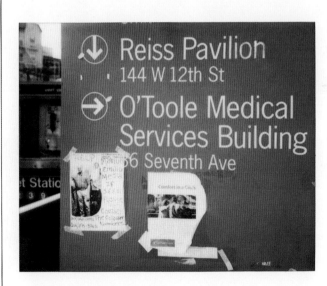

510

16

Morgue

514

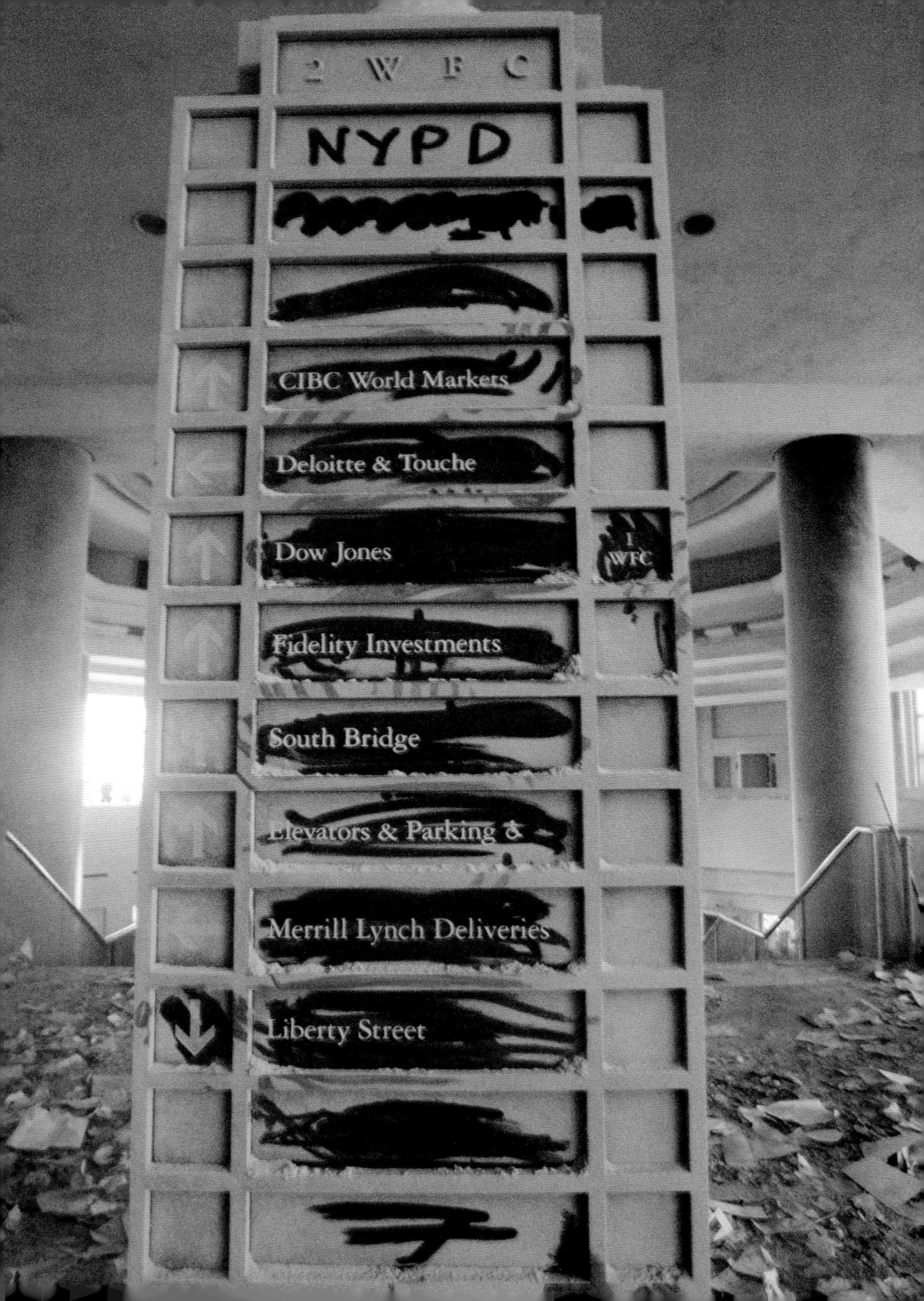
2 WFC
NYPD
CIBC World Markets
Deloitte & Touche
Dow Jones
1 WFC
Fidelity Investments
South Bridge
Elevators & Parking &
Merrill Lynch Deliveries
Liberty Street

'01 911

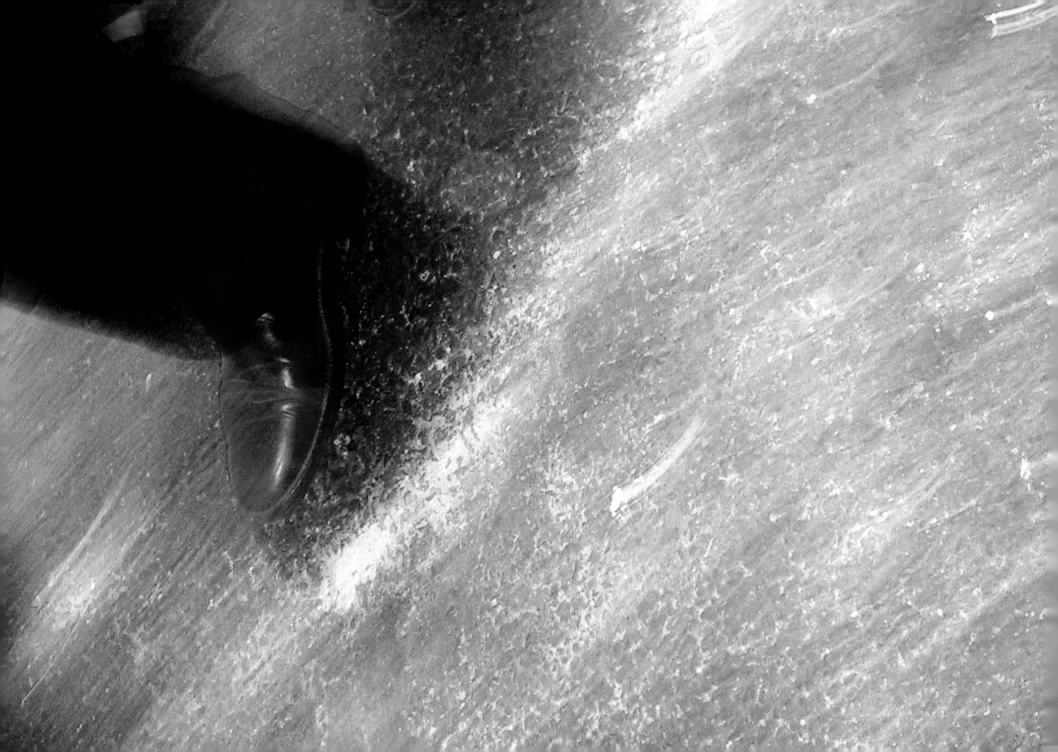

536

Finance
2 World Financial Center · 5th Floor
New York NY 10080

Merrill Lynch

541

We Are Not
Afraid.

544

548

555

559

562

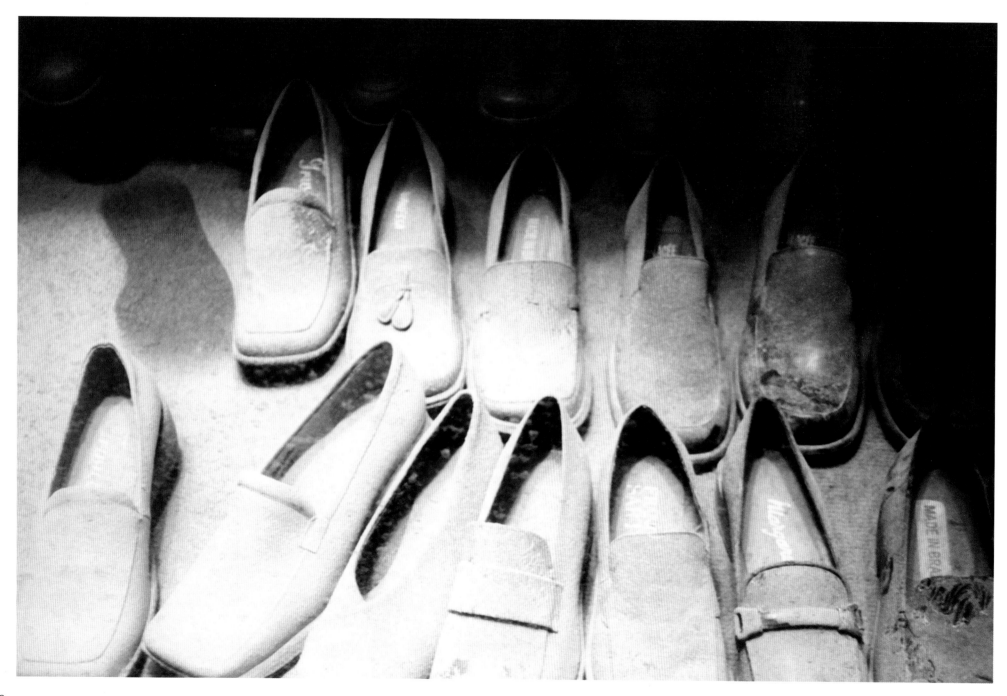

570

572

574

581

584

589

590

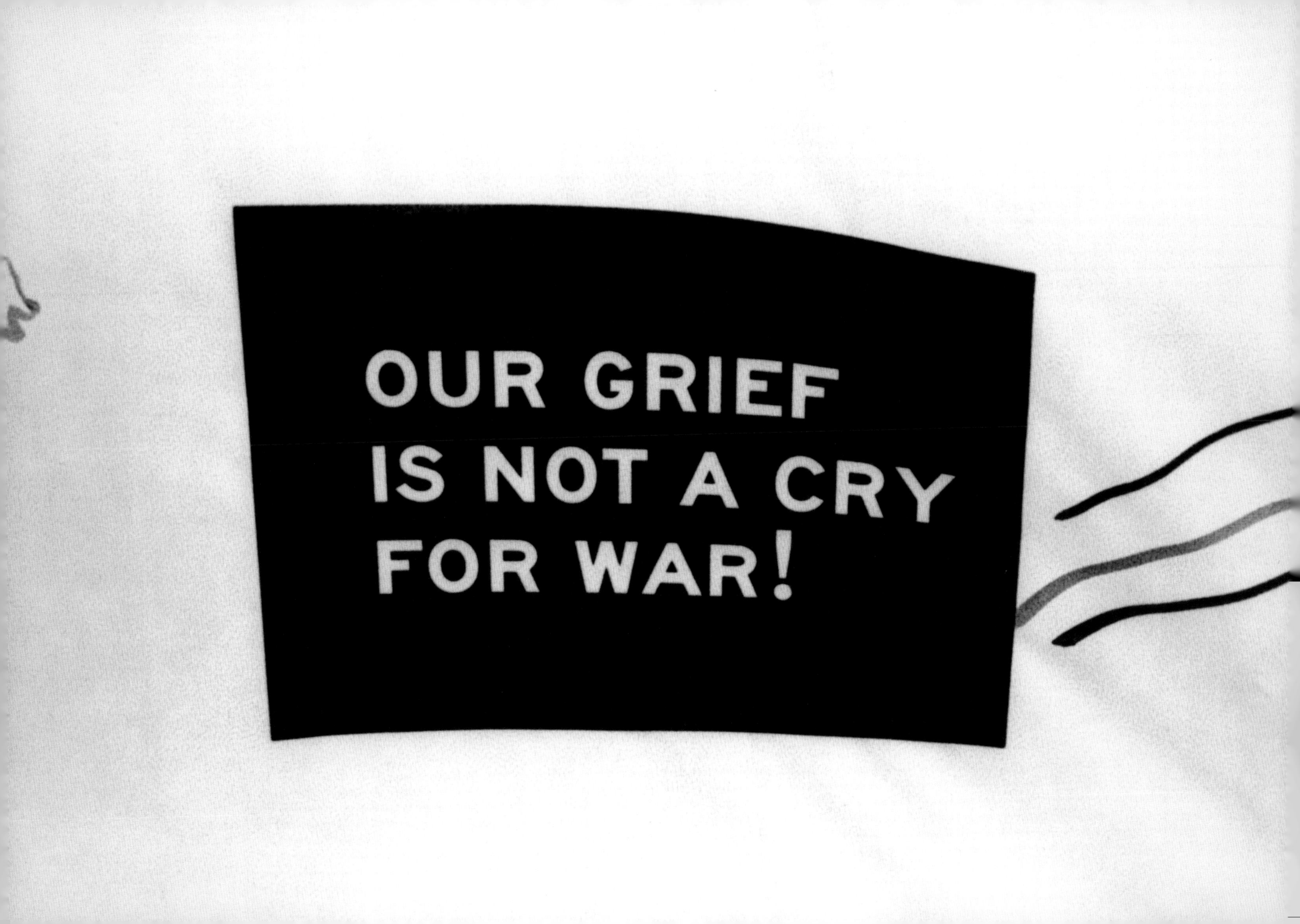
OUR GRIEF
IS NOT A CRY
FOR WAR!

sister (Tina)

...st name is Miesul
work at the compan
Espeed and Deanna G.
was the 106th Floo s o
1 Building. Her m ther ar
the Husband spoke t her
9am morning. Deanna is
32 year old and er Ht 5'4
B.D. 8/ /1969. Deanna is 30.
Pregnant and Deanna got
married July 21 2001.
Deanna have Hazel eyes
Brown Hair and he have
maybe carring an inhale

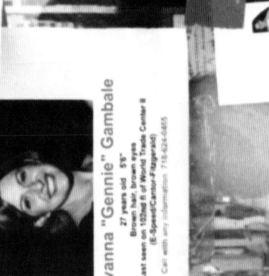

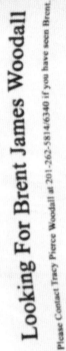

KEEFE, BRUYETTE & WOOD EMPLOYEE
IF YOU HAVE ANY INFORMATION PLEASE
CALL: 631-549-5595

AGE: 25   HT: 6'   WT: 170

Adam Rand
F.D.N.Y. Squad 288

5'5" - 200lbs.
Light Eyes
Dark Blonde Hair
Scar on Left Index Finger

Any Information Please Call
Squad 288 - (718) 476 - 6288

MISSING
Joseph Riverso
World Trade Center Tower 1
Cantor Fitzgerald 103rd Floor

Age: 37
Height: 5'9" - Wei
Hair, Brown
Eyes, Bro
Employed by Mars
Position: Acc

NYU, Class of 1987: Stern

If you have talked to or see
Mr. & Mrs. A. Russo at (9

John F. Puckett

John F. Puckett
24 Titus Road
Glen Cove, NY

General Description: Tall, slender, glasses
Thinning light brown hair, distorted thumb on left hand

John is assumed to last seen setting up the
audio for a conference/meeting at
Windows on the World on the 106th floor of Building 1 WTC.
John was wearing a black suit, white shirt & tie.

MISSING
ne World Trade Center, 100th Floor

Height: 5' 8"
Weight: 185 lbs.
Hair: Brown
w/ grey beard
Eyes: Blue
Age: 53

Roger Mark Rasweiler
(a.k.a., R. Mark Rasweiler
or Mark Rasweiler)

Any information, please call
908-782-4986 or 908-303-5345
or 908-303-5344

MISSING

Joseph Reina — 32 Years old, 240lbs, 5 feet 10
brown eyes, brown hair.

He has an eagle tattoo on his right arm & a tribal band
tattoo on his left arm. He was wearing a black shirt &
black pants. He wears a gold & dimond wedding band
on his left hand.
He worked for Cantor Fitzgerald on the 101st floor of
tower one. If anyone knows anything please call
Lisa @ 718-227-6458

HAVE YOU SEEN JOHN?

NAME   JUAN (A.K.A. JOHN) WILLIAM RIVERA
DOB   10-8-73 (27 YRS OLD)
HEIGHT   5'10
WEIGHT   185 LBS
EYES   DARK BROWN
HAIR   DARK BROWN - SHORT IN A CAESAR HAIRCUT
FACIAL   GOATEE
MARKS   SCAR ON HIS SCALP THAT IS HEALING FROM A RECENT CAR ACCIDENT

DESCRIPTION OF CLOTHING
HE WAS WEARING A BURGUNDY SHIRT WITH BEIGE HORIZONTAL LINES, BEIGE
KHAKI PANTS, BURGUNDY AND BEIGE TIMBERLAND BOOTS.

WORK INFO.   GENERAL TELECOM (GenTel)
             NORTH TOWER OF THE WTC ON THE 83RD FLOOR
             (FACING NEW JERSEY)

IF YOU HAVE ANY INFORMATION REGARDING JOHN'S STATUS, PLEASE CALL
       LILLIAN (SISTER) (917) 209-8569
       YVONNE (AUNT) (917) 488-8969
       MAHRII (FRIEND) (718) 842-2163

FOR MORE UP TO DATE INFORMATION PLEASE REFER TO

http://www.geocities.com/johnwtc2001

HAVE YOU SE
5'8, 140 LBS., BR

LAST SEEN 9/11/01

2 WORLD TRADE
PLEASE CALL IF
845-634-9215, 201-

ISSING
id Pruim

r the
WTC

Possibly seen
outside the
WTC after
the crash.

6+ ft. tall
Heavy set
Blonde
Pale Skinned
Wedding band

MISSING

Everett M. Proctor 44yrs old, 5ft 10inches
190lbs. blue eyes. light brown hair. has a tattoo
the shape of a heart.

Everett M. Proctor worked on the 103rd floor WTC tower 1 for
Cantor Fitzgerald. If you have any information on him
please contact (718) 792-0426 or (917) 561-6694

MISSING PERSON : WTC # 1

Ehtesham Raja
Age: 28
Height: 5' 10"
Hair Color: Black
Eyes: Black
Contact Phone # 518-475-7987

SHREYAS RANGANATH
CONTACT:
201-966-6961
917-921-6418

HELP US LOOK FOR
ANTHONY PEREZ

AGE-33 D.O.B 3-31-68 EMPLOYER: Candor
Fitzgerald E-Speed, had ID Badge. Was on
103rd FL ONEWorld Trade Center. 6'1" 180
LBS. Brown hair and eyes. No birth marks or
tatoos. Wife-MaryGola-Perez (516) 656-0289
Parents-Antonio&MariaPerez(516)889-8374.
Wearing docker pants-grey pullover.

ISSING IN T.

Height: 5.2
Weight: 143lbs.
Age: 29 yrs.

Missing.

Moises Rivas

g Loved One,

CARMEN MILAGROS RODRIGUEZ (MILLIE)

AGE: 46
HAIR: OWN (below shoulder)
WEIGHT: DR LBS.
HEIGHT: #55
EMPLOYER: AON, INC. (92ND FLOOR)
BLOOD TYPE: 0+
LAST SEEN: 9-11-01 on 78TH FLOOR
SKIN: OLIVE SKIN (SUN TAN)
RACE: HISPANIC

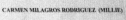

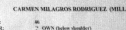

Attention Firemen, Policemen, and Rescue Workers.

Our Spa Facilities / Services are available for your disposal, free of charge.

Facilities / Services : restroom, showers, basic massages, refreshments, lounge

Eden Day Spa
388 Broadway
New York, NY 10013
(212) 226-0515

MISSING
since Monday, Sep 10 2001
. Sneha Ann Philip, M.D.

Hair, Brown Eyes
5 lbs
Skin
ars old

Please call with ANY information
Ron Lieberman: 917-825-7566
Ashwin Philips: 202-494-8734
sneha@imagilab.com

Last seen wearing a brown collared short-sleeved dress that
goes down to her knees with buttons down the front
Shoes: brown loafers

Missing from WTC
Diane Parsons
DOB 7-14-43
5'3 ,145 lbs, Blnd Hair, Grn Eyes
Please Call (518) 441-4852
(518) 899-5938
From Albany NY Area- NYS Tax

IF YOU HAD ANY CONTACT WITH MICH
WHEREABOUTS IN TH

Anyone with any information please call 201 86

ISLAM IS NOT THE ENEMY.
WAR IS NOT THE ANSWER.
LET'S WORK TO END
THE CYCLE. PASS IT ON...

614

617

630

632

637

638

654

655

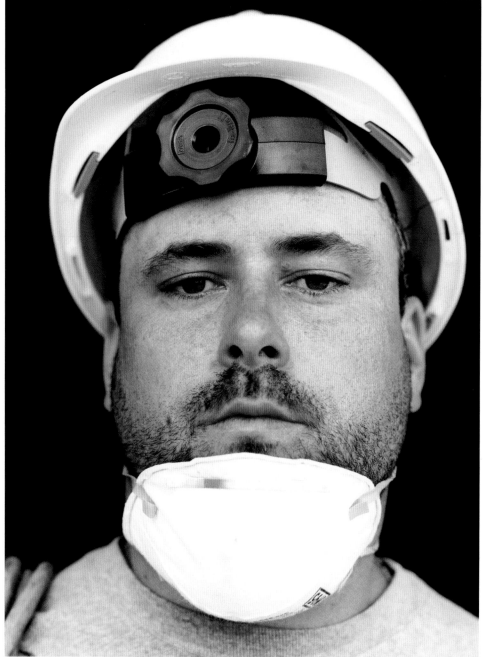

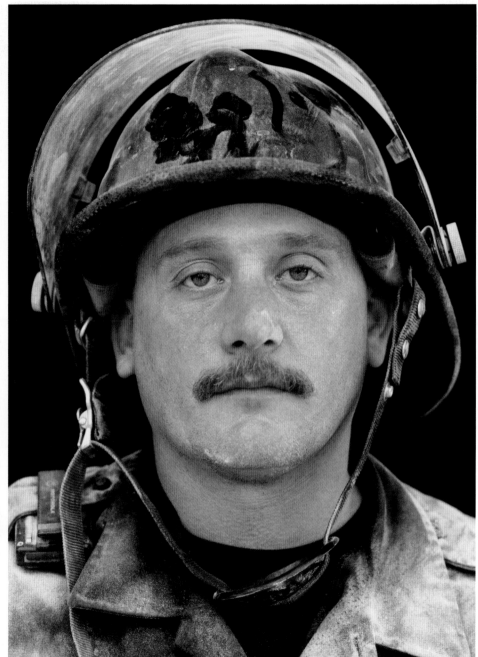

668

680

684

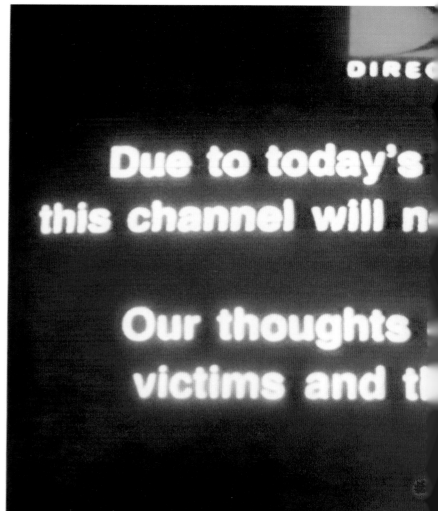

698

MISSING BROTHER

Y GEORGE LATOUCHE

715

716

718

720

722

723

726

727

735

744

747

MISSING
Tonyell McDay

Tonyell McDay was employed at Marsh technologies in Tower 1. She's African American, 25 yrs. old. DOB 6/24/76. She's approx. 5'4, 130 lb. she has long dk. brown hair, and dk brown eyes. She's wearing a ruby ring on her right ring finger and a college ring on her right ring finger. She is also her left pinky finger and a silver ring on her left pinky finger and an anklet. She has on a silver finger from Jersey City State college. She has on a silver wearing gold jewelry and an anklet. We're extremely worried about her!!!!!! fossil watch.

Maybe someone has seen her.

If you have any information, please call The McDay Family at 732-499-7118 or 732-388-7785.

756

763

785

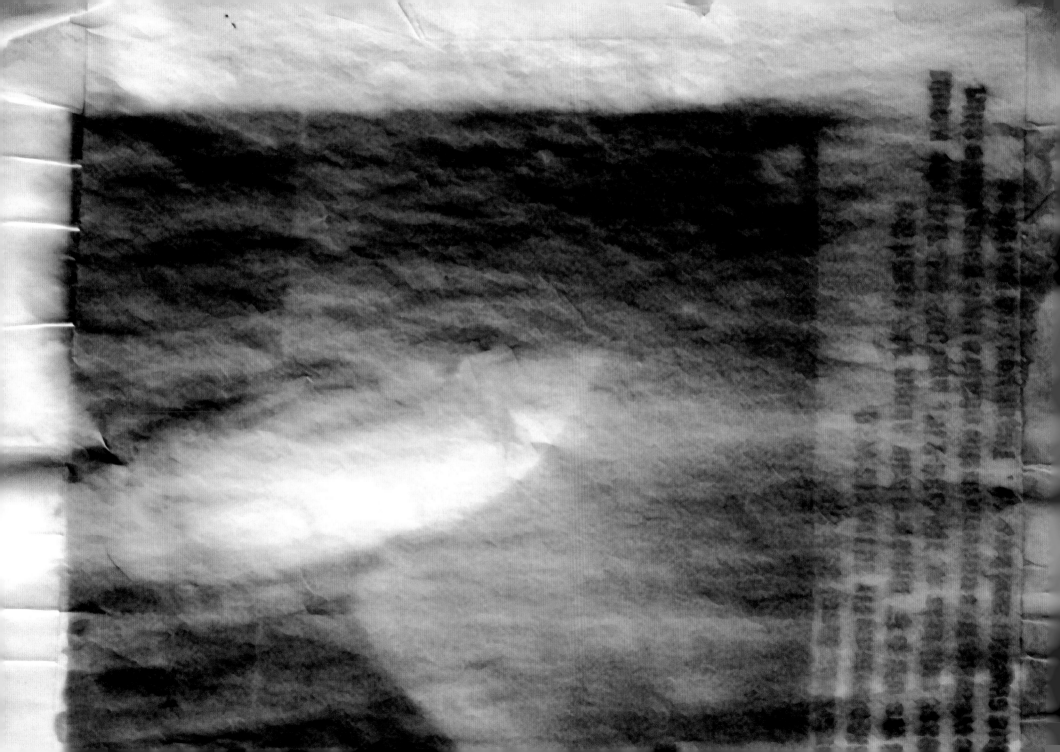

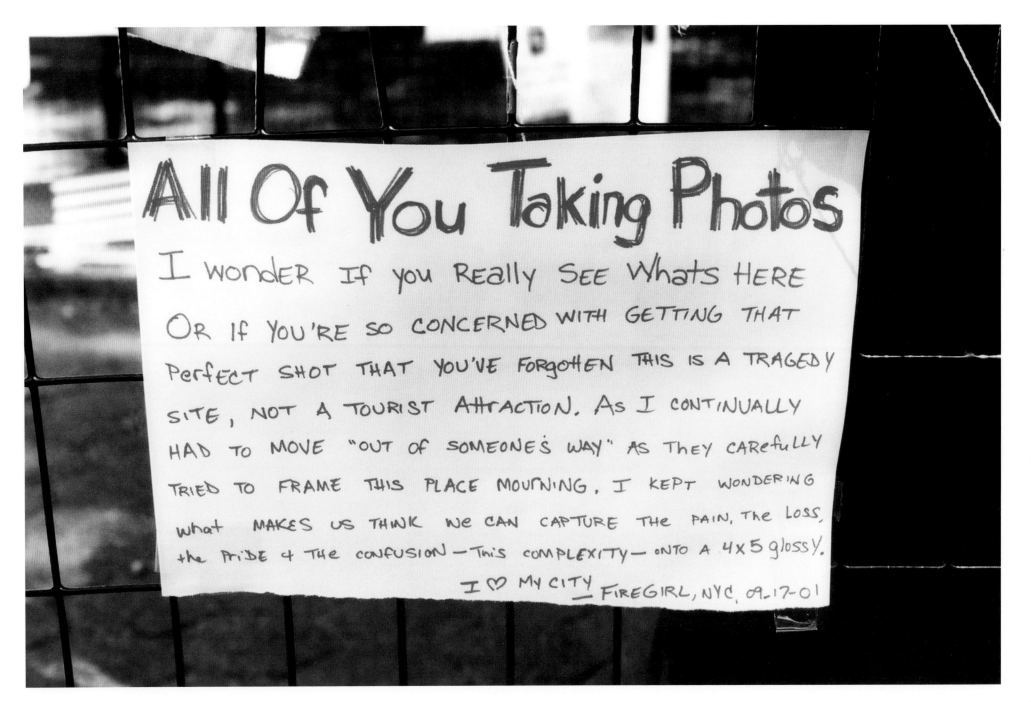

here is new york **timeline**

september 2001

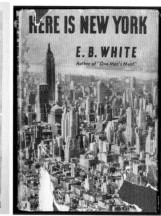

SEPT 12 Picture #0000, a flea-market photograph of the World Trade Center, is hung in the window of the vacant shop at 116 Prince Street.

SEPT 15–24 The organizers plan the exhibition, collecting equipment, enlisting volunteers, and soliciting pictures from magazines and newspapers. School of Visual Arts students put a splash page on the internet calling for submissions.

SEPT 25 *here is new york* opens to the public with a few dozen photographs, which are clipped to wires without frames or names. The closing date is announced as October 14.

834

october

OCT 2 As submissions mount, sales volunteers begin taking orders for prints, all of which are to be sold for $25. The plan is to fill orders on the spot, using two desktop printers borrowed from volunteers.

OCT 9 Roberta Smith reviews the exhibition in the *New York Times*, followed the next day by Vince Aletti's review in the *Village Voice*.

OCT 12 As submissions continue to pour in, the storefront at 116 Prince Street is literally filled to the ceiling. Shiseido Cosmetics (America), Ltd., which controls the lease to the vacant storefront next door at 118 Prince Street, agrees to lend the space to the exhibition. The key is obtained at 4 p.m. At 6 p.m., the second storefront has been hung with pictures and is opened to the public.

OCT 13 A telephone is finally installed in the original storefront, one day before the exhibition is scheduled to close.

OCT 14 The exhibition is extended until October 28.

OCT 15 There is now a one-month backlog of print orders.

OCT 16 Worldwide coverage by Beth Nissen on CNN.

OCT 22 Media attention increases, with articles in the *Washington Post* and other newspapers worldwide. *The Newshour*, *The Today Show*, *World News Tonight*, and *Dateline* run major reports about the exhibition.

OCT 23 FEMA begins process of examining images for their engineering report on the collapse of the Twin Towers.

OCT 26 A trailer truck delivers 40 desktop printers to 116 Prince Street.

OCT 28 With long lines of people still waiting to see the show, the exhibition is extended until Thanksgiving.

OCT 30 Philip Coltoff, Executive Director and Chief Executive Officer of the Children's Aid Society, acknowledges receipt of the first $100,000 from *here is new york*.

november

NOV 1 Organizers honored by the Children's Aid Society, at their Harlem facility.

NOV 2 here is new york is established as a 501(c)(3) not-for-profit corporation.

NOV 5 The Horace W. Goldsmith Foundation donates $100,000 for equipment and infrastructure.

NOV 8 A party for volunteers is held at Canteen Restaurant in Soho.

NOV 10 Track 16 Gallery in Santa Monica hosts a 300-print show

NOV 13 Project organizers and volunteers visit Ground Zero.

NOV 15 A Plexiglas and Mylar screen is fabricated and hung in the window of 116 Prince Street; images are projected onto it 24 hours a day.

NOV 18 A 200-print exhibition opens at the School of Journalism, University of California at Berkeley.

NOV 24 The New York exhibition is extended until Christmas.

DEC 1 The backlog of print orders is now two months.

DEC 5 A reception for the staff and the neighborhood is held in both storefronts and at the Mimi Ferzt Gallery next door.

DEC 17 Benefit for *here is new york* is held at the studio of Diane von Furstenberg, sponsored by *The Week* magazine.

DEC 20 Web catalog inaugurated with some 1500 pictures.

DEC 23 Former President William Jefferson Clinton visits.

DEC 24 A tarp is hung across the windows of the storefronts; the exhibition closes.

DEC 25 A Christmas party for staff and friends is held at 116 Prince Street.

DEC 26–JAN 2 Crowds continue to gather outside the storefronts at all hours, watching the electronic display and seeking admittance.

january 2002

JAN 2 The exhibition reopens on a reduced schedule, now open 5 days a week instead of 7.

JAN 10 The e-commerce version of www.hereisnewyork.org is inaugurated, allowing the images to be sold online.

here is hope
devastation life
death shock horror
unity heroism fear
disbelief anger love
courage sadness
grief compassion
spirit new york

february

FEB 1 Target sponsors a 1500-print exhibition at the Chicago Cultural Center.

FEB 12 The International Center of Photography and the Durst Organization provide *here is new york* with a new space at 1105 Sixth Avenue for an exhibition encompassing both WTC pictures and photographs from Afghanistan, the Middle East, and New York City since 9/11.

FEB 28 The Museum of Modern Art opens a new photography exhibition, *Life In The City*, which is partly inspired by *here is new york* and features two electronic projections of its images.

march

MARCH 1 The backlog of print orders has been cleared.

MARCH 11 Mayor Richard M. Daley visits *here is new york*'s Chicago installation.

MARCH 21 www.hereisnewyork.org registers more than 200 million hits.

MARCH 31 Another $100,000 is donated to the Children's Aid Society, bringing the total to $600,000.

april

APRIL 1 A party for the contributing photographers is held at 1105 Sixth Avenue and the International Center of Photography. A group photo of some 600 of those present is taken in Grace Plaza at 10 p.m. A slideshow of 80 selected images from the exhibition runs for an hour on the giant Panasonic Astrovision screen in Times Square.

APRIL 4 Panel discussion about *here is new york* is conducted at the International Center of Photography.

APRIL 9 *voices of 9.11*, a new video project inviting photographers and others who were at Ground Zero to record oral histories, opens at 1105 Sixth Avenue.

may

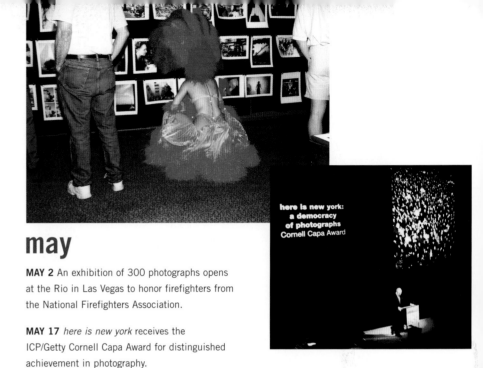

MAY 2 An exhibition of 300 photographs opens at the Rio in Las Vegas to honor firefighters from the National Firefighters Association.

MAY 17 *here is new york* receives the ICP/Getty Cornell Capa Award for distinguished achievement in photography.

june

JUNE 26 This book is delivered to Switzerland for printing.

Pictures in this section by were contributed by David Allee, Maggie Berkvist, Chris Cawley, Paul Constantine, Katja Heinemann, Paul Manes, Brenda English Manes, Jay Manis, Lara McPherson, Sam Meyers, Edwin Mullon, Jeff Rutzky, Michael Shulan.

exhibitions to date

Sept. 25, 2001 through Sept. 29, 2002
116 Prince Street, New York, NY

Nov. 10–Dec. 8, 2002
Track 16 Gallery, Santa Monica, CA

Nov. 18–Dec. 21, 2001
University of California, Berkeley, CA

Feb. 1–March 30, 2002
Chicago Cultural Center, Chicago, IL

Feb. 12–June 1, 2002
International Center of Photography, New York, NY

Feb. 22–May 19, 2002
Southeast Museum of Photography,
Daytona Beach, FL

Feb. 28–May 21, 2002
Museum of Modern Art, New York, NY

May 2–May 9, 2002
Uniformed Firefighters Assoc., Las Vegas, NV

July 5–Oct. 7, 2002
Martin-Gropius-Bau, Berlin, Germany

July 6–Aug. 18, 2002
Les Rencontres d'Arles, Arles, France

Sept. 3–Oct. 4, 2002
Rathaus Stuttgart, Stuttgart, Germany

Sept. 3–Oct. 4,2002
Zurich Kunsthaus, Zurich, Switzerland

Sept. 3–Oct. 31, 2002
Free Public Library, Louisville, KY

Sept. 4–Sept. 30, 2002
Fulton Street Gallery, Troy, NY

Sept. 4–Sept. 27, 2002
Marietta College, McDonough Center, Andrews Hall,
Marietta, OH

Sept. 5–Oct. 31, 2002
Fotofest, Houston, TX

Sept. 7–Nov. 11, 2002
Corcoran Gallery of Art, Washington, D.C.

Sept. 9–Oct. 8, 2002
Grand Court at International Plaza and Bay Street, Tampa, FL

Sept. 10–Nov. 10, 2002
232 Fifth Avenue, San Diego, CA

Sept. 10–Oct. 30, 2002
Fourth Presbyterian Church, Chicago, IL

Sept. 10–Sept. 17, 2002
Mitsukoshi, Chou-Ku, Tokyo, Japan

Sept. 10–Oct. 31, 2002
The Sausage Factory, Dublin, Ireland

Sept. 11–Oct. 6, 2002
NRW-Forum Kultur und Wirtschaft, Duesseldorf, Germany

Sept. 11–Oct. 5, 2002
The Newsroom, London, England

Sept. 11–Sept. 20, 2002
85-87, Rue du Fubourg-Saint-Martin, Paris, France

Sept. 11–Sept. 30, 2002
The Richard Stockton College of New Jersey, Pomona, NJ

Sept. 11–Nov. 15, 2002
Florida Atlantic University, Boca Raton, FL

October 2002
Dresdner Druck-Verlagshaus – Saechsische Zeitung,
Dresden, Germany

for updated information, please consult our website
www.hereisnewyork.org

here is new york
staff spring
2002

Jeanine Assogba

Martha K. Babcock

Maggie Berkvist

Chris Cawley

Clete Christopher

Paul Constantine

Abigail Feldman

Michael Glowik

Kevin Goggin

Pamela Griffiths

Mary Liao

Mark Lubell

Tim Main

Brenda English Manes

Jay Manis

Lara McPherson

Juan Molinari

Edward Mullon

Sam Myers

Luisa Santos

Deborah Schwartz

Stephanie Schenppe

Ruth Sergel

Fernanda Matarazzo Suplicy

Aaron Traub

Mary Traub

Daniel Valdez

Suzanne Williamson

Bilal Zaidi

photographers

Monika Abate
Joan Abbey
Michael Abdi
Craig Abel
Troy Abel
John Abela
Rachel Abesamis
Tevin Abeshouse
Josh Abrams
Tim Abshire
Jenny Acheson
Terry Ackerman
Sean Thomas Ackley 79
Santi-Jose Acosta
Jack Adams
Jeff Adams
John Adams
Lea Adams
Helen Adelman
Joree Adilman
Denise Jones Adler
Carole Adrian
Samantha Aezen
Ron Agam 358, 782
Norma Agatstein
Gianni Agostinelli
Christophe Agou 420, 421, 518
Javier Agredo
Rick Aguilar
Darius Aidala
Joanne Ainsworth
Erika Alabarca
William Alatriste 533, 546, 547, 548, 549
Maryse Alberti 672
Cristina Albino
Teri Alcabes
Jared Alechman
Luis Alejandro-Carpio
Heidi Alexander
Angelis Alexandris 346
William Alger

Boni C. Alimagno
David Allee 828, 829
David Young Allen
Lisa Allen
Renate Aller 224
Richard Aloisio
Barbara Alper
Lawrence John Altman
Rita Altman
Larry Amanuel
Marc Ameruso
Lotem Ami
Kevin Amter
Randy Anagnostis 631
Chris Anderson
Roy Anderson 493
Stephen Anderson
Frank Andolino
Eric Andrus 362
Geoffrey Anenberg
Michele Angerosi
Garrett Anglin
Monica Ani 655
Nir Antebi
Catherine Anthenien
Anita Antonini
H. Aoki
Cindy Aponte
M. Apparition
Ariel Apte
Nunzio Aquilino
Ervin R. Aquina
Adolf Aragon
Shigeko Arai
Jessica Arana
Ronald Arbouet
Elizabeth Archangeli
Jerry Arcieri 2, 32, 33, 87
Melissa Arden-Wong 262, 337
Luis Banuelos Arechiga
Roy Arenella
Robert J. Arens Jr.

Jeanne Arfanis
Gustavo Aristizabac
Ann Arlen
Babs Armour
Larry Armour
Bill Armstrong 395
Dianne Arndt
Christopher C. Arnold
James Arnold
Rebecca Arnold
Madeleine Hope Arthurs 821
Leandro Artigala
Andrea Artz 542
Kristi Ash
Dan Asher
Eli Ashkenazi 335
Carole Ashley
Brian Ashley-White
Fred Askew
Kimberly Atlas
Alice Attie
Jane Evelyn Atwood 556, 707, 774, 775
Jeffrey Auger
Margherita Auletta
Jill Avalon
Noema Avila
Michaly Ayervais
Jeannine Ayres
Anna Azarov
Ross Babbit 480
Martha Babcock
Luca Babini
Zsolt Bacai
Brian Bachisin
Barbara Backer
Stephanie Badini
Christine Badowski
Kathleen Bailey
Michael Bailey
Richard Bajornas
Ryan Bakerink

Nelson Bakerman
Gordon L. Baldwin
Stefan C. Ballard
Anna Banaszak
Stanley Banos
Robert Barber 231
Joel Barcelona
Steven Bard
Lisa Barlow
Tom Barlow
Diana E. Barnett
Briony Barr
Jane Barrer 188
Annie Barrett
Chuck Barrett
Jim Barrett
Megan Barron 98, 99
Ted Barron
Rita Barros
Susan Barrow
Olivia Barry
Gregory Bartkus
Sally Barton
Daniel Bartosik
Marc Basch
Carolyn Bassani
Donna Bassin
Christine Bastoni
Muhaideen Batah
Ananda Bates 312
Stacey Battenfield
Eric Baum
Erica Baum
M. Justin Baum
Susan Bauman
Elaine Bauman
Sihan Bazzy
Liza Bear
Kevin Beatovic
Bill Beatty
Karen Beatty
Kevin Beauchamp

Gustavo Bechini
Steven Beck
Chris Becker
Erica Becker
John Becker
Nick Beckett
Valerie Beckford
Andrea Beckley
Claire Beckman 240
Marek Beczek
Bryan Bedder
James Beeler
Lore Behrendt
Sascha Beicken
Sascha Beiken
Michael Beirne 804
Maureen Beitlerm 132, 136
Esther Beke
Sarah Bellamy
Andrew Belletty
Thompson Bellingrath
Sarah Bellows
Kelley Bellucci
Mario Belluomo
Nick Belton
Antin Bendersky
Marian Benes 38
Nicole Bengiveno
Matt Benson
Tracy Benson
A. Bensusen
Georgine Benvenuto 366, 367
John Berchtold
Nancy Berchtold
Csaba Bereczky 543
Andrew Berends
Frits Berends
Karin Bereson
Alexander Berg
Gretchen Berg
Amy Bergenfeld
Beth Anne Berger

Erica Berger
Melissa Berger 856
Michael Berger
Stephanie Berger
Nicholas Bergery
Richard Bergman 683
Ed Bergstraesser
Pamela Berkovic
Maggie Berkvist
David Berkwitz
Miriam Berman
Nina Berman 72
Robby Berman
Joan Berman-Goldberg
Francois Bernadi
Nancy Bernhaut 733
J. Scott Berniker
William Berns
Elizabeth Bernstein
Judy Bernstein
Meredith Bernstein
Lee Berresford
Victoria Berrios
Ryan Beshera
Alberto Betancourt
Petra Beter
Giuseppe Bianco
Christopher Bickford
Holger Biermann
Claude Biet
Todd Bigelow 372, 373
William Biggart
Nancy C. Bilas
Allan Bilodeau
E. Birnbaum
Maclean Ports Bishop 680, 681
Meredith Bitzer
Andy Black
Vincent Blackhawk-Aamodt
Mark L. Blackshear
Ann Blackstock
Diane Bladecki

Patricia Blaho
Christian Blair
Bethel Blakesley
James Blanchard
Frances Blanche 204, 205
Ana Blanco
Nathan Blaney
Gil Blank
Arnelle Blas
Daniel Blas
Julie Blattberg 95
Jonathan Blaustein
Dianne Blell
Jacob Blickenstaff 126a, 127a
Beth Block
Carol Block
Lois Block
Karen Blood
Sandra Bloodworth
Edward Bloom
Sid Blustain
Anjali Bn
Philip Boag
Phyllis Bobb
Ana Carolina Boclin
Sandra Boer
Neill Bogan
Valerie Bolger
Marko Bon
Tacitus Bond
Lea Bonnier
Santina Bono
Andrea Booher 84, 386, 387, 388, 389, 391, 729
Jonathan Bookallil
Elsa Borrero 812
Christopher Bosch 342
Peter Bosch
Mary Boss
Ron Boszko
Friederike Bothe
Lisa Rosa Bottone

Jeanine Boubli 740a
Veronique Boufy
Jean-Christian Bourcart
Mijanou Bourdelon
Dexter Bowen
Robert Bowen 214
Susan Bowen
Margot Boyd
Thomas K.E. Boyd
Robert Boyer III 563
Chris Boyle
Stephen Boyle
Tim Brace 414
David Bradford 20
Diane Bradshaw
James Brady
Gregory Brail
Brad Brailsford
John Branch 824
George Brand
Damon Brandt
Colleen Branigan
Rebecca Brasseur
Dee Breger
Andrea Bregoff
Brenda Brenner
Brandon Brewer
Christophe D. Brewer
Ingrid Breyer
Michael Brian
William Bridge
Allison Bridges
Louis Briendel
Kaye Brinker
Zana Briski 174
David Britton
Kristen Brochmann
Beverly Brodsky
Lara Brodzinsky
Kyle R. Brooks 569
Pauletta Brooks
Yvonne Brooks

Amy Brown
Christopher Brown 466
Daniel Brown
Everen Brown
Ken Brown 512
Malcolm Brown
Michael Brown
Richard V. Brown
Aaron Browne
Christine Brownlee
J. Gavin Bruce
Jay Bruff
Steve Bryant
Daniel Brysacz
Lisa Buchner
Elaine Buchsbaum
Erik Buck
Michael Buckley
Jane Buckwalter
Jim Budman
Michael V. Budzinski
Phillip Buehler 800, 802
Melinda Buie
Helen Bullock
Amy B. Burchenal
Szu Burgess
Wendy Burgreen
Garvin Burke
Pete Burke 479
Cyndie Burkhardt
Tom Burnett 220
Moshe Bursuker
Santiago Busamante
Katherine Busch
Else Buschheuer
Laurie Butler
Patrick Butler
David Button
Dottie Buyher
Colby Buzzell
Gary Byrne 104
William Byrnes 531

Limarie Cabrera 463
Mario Cabrera
Mark Caccavo
Mo Cahill
Virginia Cahill
Susan Callahan 756
Chris Callis 846
Kike Calvo
Andrew J. Camacho 234
Larry Cameola
John Caminiti
John Caminitti
Kathie Cammann
Eric Campbell
Michele Campo
Marco Campos
Michael Canavan
Davide Cantoni
Martine Capalbo
Michael Capone
Thomas Caravaglia
M. Carbonaro
Dawn Carey 589
Kelly Carleton
Marie-Helene Carleton
Patricia Carlisle
Emily Carlson
Danny Carlton
Flora Carnevale
Claudine Caro
Jeff Carpenter
Luis Carpio
Gable Carr
Hector Carrasquillo
Domingo Carro
Nancy Carroll
Patricia Carroll
Sarah Carroll
Charlie Carson 225
Andres Carter
William J. Carter
Antrim Caskey 39, 398, 399

Joseph Cassar
Michael Casserly
Sean Casserly
Sean Cassidy
Ellisa Cassuto
George Castanis
Jordi Castellsague
Anaiza Castro Valle
James Cathcart
Carol Caulfield
Gerard Cavanagh
Sean Cavanaugh
Chris Cawley **613, 725, 817**
Vittorio Celentano
Jimi Celeste
Bibi Cencik
Peter Cermak
Arzu Cevik
Anna Chadwick
Antonio Chagas
Franck Chagniot
Diego Chamorro
Michael Champlin
Lia Chang
Dan Chatman
Lisa Chau
Sheryl Checkman
Jonathon Cheetham
Flora Chen
Wei-Fang Chen
Yiling Chen-Josephson
Edward Cheng
Anita Chernewski
Myrel Chernick
Stephanie Chernikowski
Wai H. Cheung
Phyllis A. Chillingworth **313**
Thomas Chin
Alan Chin
Matt Chin
Robert K Chin
Carlo Chinca
Nikki Chokshi

Bozena Cholewa
Shui-Fong Chong **820**
Eduardo Chorro
Irene Choy
Theresa Christiansen
Lynn Christoffers
Mona Chun
Emil Chynn **748**
Howard Chynsky
Viera Cibele
Peg Ciccarelli
Frank Cina
Karen Cipolla
Joe Cirina
Bettina Cirone
George Cisneros
Peter Ciszewski **108, 109**
Jeremiah Clancy **207, 690-691**
Keith Clancy
Fernanda Clariana **504**
Aileen Clark
Gary F. Clark
Mary Pugh Clark
Nancy Clark
Holly Clarke
Diamond Clay
Robert Cleary
Laura Cleaver
Rene Clement **324, 325**
Candy Clemente
Kerry Clemons
Donna Clovis
Djamilla Rosa Cochran
Richard Coda
Aaron Cohen
Beth Cohen
Dan Cohen
Marc Cohen
Nancy Cohen
Richard Cohen **316**
Richard H. Cohen **330, 331, 783**
Seth Cohen **649**
Leita Hensen Cohn **618-619**

John Colby
Martin Cole
Michael F. Collarone **292, 293, 735**
Charles M. Collins
Jennifer Collins
Tracy Collins
Jennifer Colman
Nicole Columbus
Cynthia Colwell **213**
Jay Comella
Gabriel Comrie
Mirana Comstock
Kevin M. Coneys
Eileen Connor
Alice Connorton **511**
Cary Conover **152**
Fred R. Conrad
Conrad, Myoda, Laverdiere
Paul Constantine
Rose Marie Constantino
Amanda Cook
Jennifer H. Cooke **673**
Juli Cooper
Justine Cooper **590**
Shawne Cooper
Teresa Cooper
Jay Corcoran
Lydia Cornwall-Bishop
Erin Cornyn
Lorraine Corsale
Josef Corso **97, 135**
Lucille Corva
Eduardo Costa
Anthony Cotsifas
Natalie Coulter **686**
Karen Covey
Chojecki Cowburn
Nigel Cox **505**
Topher Cox
Gibson Craig **528, 529**
Lynn Crain
Joe Craine
Craig Cramer

Jon Creamer
Virginia Creeper
Keisha Crenshaw
Al Crespo
Victor Cretella
Luke Crisalli
Adrianne Cronas
Kenneth Crowe
Kevin Crowley
Louise Crowley
Michelle Cruz
Constanza Cuadrado
Sarah Cullen
Dell Cullum
Joyce Culver
Bruce Cunningham
Raymond Curiale
David Curry
Frank Cutler
Denise Cutter
David Cwirka **539**
Roberto D'Addona
Brian D'Aurelio
Karen D'Onofrio
Oliver Daehler **255**
Geoffrey Dahill
David Daines
Angelo Dainese
Kevin N. Daley **369**
Sam Daley
Joe Damato
Matilde Damele **60, 61**
Peter Daniti
Philip Dankner
Jonathan Dann
Jennifer Clifford Danner
Anne Darer
Isabel Daser **469**
Chris DaSilva
Linda Davey
Phillippe David
Huw Davies
Paul Davies

Robert Davies
Sally Davies **710, 711**
John F. Davis
Peter Davis
Susan Davis
Adam Day
Diane Day **746**
Steven De Castro
Pierre de Gaillante
Maria De La Ossa
Frank de Las Mercedes
Ricardo de Masi
S. DeBeyrie
Charles Debold
Kevin DeCamp
Lisa Decker
Jay Dedman
Kathy deGennaro
Tony DeGeorge
Kathy Deitch
Michael Dekker
Ariane Delacampagne
Kevin Crego Delaire
Colleen Delaney **717**
Yasmine Delawari
Blaise DelBianco
Giovanni DelBrenna **54, 55**
Sandy Dell
Jared Della Valle
Matthew Dellaccio
Dana DellaValle
Richard Dembinski
Lou Dembrow **719**
Demuth/Katz
Kenneth Denicola
Robert Derek
David Derex
Sandra DeSando
Jane Waggoner Deschner
Joseph DeSciose
Marc DeSimone
Donna DeSoto
Natalie DeSurrey

Anthony DeVito **456**
Andrew Diamond
Allison Diana
Gregory DiBisceglie
Andrew Dickerson
Anita Dickhuth
Jerry Dietl
Jon Dietrich
Louis DiGiandomenico
Madeline DiGrandi
Sandra Dillon
Evelyn Dilworth
Nicole diMella
Anthony Dimino
Mikhail Dinershteyn
Anthony Dinoff
Jim DiPiazza
Daniel DiScala
Barbara Distler
Pablo Dizeo
Andrei Dmitrichev
Linda Dobhansky
Gregory Doerge
Patrick Dolan
Corinne Dolle
Philippe Dollo
Francis Domitrovich
Linda Domsky
Benjamin Donaldson **454, 455, 701**
Donald Donin
Jennifer Dooley
Maria Doppelbauer
Joanne Doroshow
Tony Dougherty
Simon P. Ferraro Dove
Megan Doyle
Nancy Drago
Robert Draizen
William Drakert **476, 477**
Jackman Draper
Pete Dressel **306**
A.M. Dropick
Michael Dubin

Rod Dubitsky **777**
Douglas Dubler
Richard DuBois
Ian Dudley
Samuel Dufaux **679**
Hilary Duffy
Kathleen Duffy
Pierre Dufour
Gary Dunkin **393**
Cheryl Dunn **581**
Richard Dunn
Catherine Dunning
Tony Dunovsky
Michel Dupras
Eugene Durante
William Duryea
Ian Dutton
Dan Dwornik
Michael Dwyer
Leigh Ann Dykes
Jeff Dyksterhouse **658-659**
Michael Ann Easton
Todd Eberle
James Eberly
Jerrilyn Eckardt
Adam Eckstrom
Aristide Economopoulos **294, 295, 296, 297, 298, 299, 382, 383, 384, 385**
Paradis Efthimios
Susan Egan
Jennifer Eggleston
Joanne Ehrie
Thom Eichinger **527**
Carmen Einfinger
Nancy Einhorn
Aryn Ekstedt
Christopher Elam
Susan Elefant
Lindsey Elenson
David Elinson
Jim Elliott
David Emmons
Cynthia Endredy **772**

Jill Enfield
Ken Eng
David Engel
Katia Engel
Marion Engelbach-Ennis
Elke Enkeboll
Joy Episalla
Bernhard Erda
Alexandra Ervell
Blossom Esainko
Johan Esbensen
Charles Eshelman
Holly Essler
Lynn Estomin
James Estrin
Barbara Ethan
Scott Ettin
Dennis Evangelatus
Guy Evans
Jeffrey B. Evans **791**
Mike Evans
Orly Even
Bettina Ewing
Gary Fabiano **278, 285, 397, 826, 827**
Timothy Fadek **623, 751**
Brendan Fagan
Lisa Fain **591**
Evan Fairbanks **498, 575, 636**
Roland Fajardo
Cyril Fakiri
Richard Falco
Daniel Falgerho
Maureen Fan
Daniel Fanelli
Brenda Fann
Nathan Farb
Enid Farber **432**
George Farinacci **115, 168, 169, 173**
Samantha Farinella
Carter Farmer
James Farrell
Melody Farrin
Jeffry Fasano

Samantha Faunce
Emmanuel Faure
William Faustner
Aaron Fedor
Rainer Fehringer
David Fein
Eric Feinberg
Richard Feinson
Art Feldman
Abigail Feldman
Art Feldman
Lisa Feldman
Matt Feldman
Erik Feldmann
Lucy Fellowes
Susan N. Felsher
Joanne Felty
Lisa Fenger
Kerin Ferallo
A Stewart Ferebee
James Ferguson
JD Ferguson
Linda Ferguson
Juanjo Fernandez
Dave Ferris
Lothar Fidelis
Laura Fieber-Minogue
Lisa Fiel
Marc Fields
Rick Figueroa
Mark Curtis Filstrup
Anne Fink
Kathryn Fink
Brian Finke **122, 123**
Alan Finkel
Madison Finlay
Anthony Fioravanti Jr.
Dominick Fiorille **410, 766**
John P. Fiorito
Robert Fisch
Christine Fiscina
Karen Fisher
Stephen Fisher

Will Fisher
Chuck Fishman **788**
Mike Fitelson
M. June Flanders
David Fleischer
Francine Fleischer
Regina Y. Fleming **753**
Susan Flis
Cesar Florez
Laura Florman
Joe Floto
Lucien Flotte
Jo An Flower
Tommy Flynn
Iris Fodor
Pete Foley
Peter Foley **280, 354, 355, 374, 422b,
779, 781**
Debbie Fong
Nicole Fontanelle
Ronald Force **26**
Ami Forchielli
Jennifer Ford
Adam Forgash **167**
Julie Anne Forgione
David Forrest
Paul Forsman
Anthony Foschino
Ahron R. Foster
Glenn Foster **45, 334, 815**
Jimmy Fountain **436**
Maria Fountoukis **403**
Frank Fournier
William Fowler
Flo Fox
Brien Foy
Robert P. Frail
Jason Francisco
Tiffani Francisco
Angel Franco
Jesse Frank
Paul Frankenstein
Harald Franzen **360**

Nathaniel David Frazier
Mike Freeburg **470**
Jed Freeman
Pilar Freire
Ruth Fremson
Olivier French
Katherine Freygang
Daniel Fried
Gabriela Fried
Beatrice Friedli
Carol Friedman
James Friestad
Etienne Frossard
James Frost
Miyoko Fukushima
Ka Lai Fung
John Funk
Karen Furth
Phillip Galgian
R. Galinsky
Greg Gallant
Joseph Gallo
Paula Galloway
Robert Gamba
Andrew Gandelman
Donna Garcia
Deborah Gardner
Micah Garen
Amy Garey
Andrew Garn **656**
Michele Garner
Anthony Gasparro
Alan Golin Gass
Jennifer Gass
James B. Gavenus
Christopher Gay
Mara Clarice Gay
James Geer
Matthew Geer
Asya Geisberg **537**
Edgar Gelabert
Bonnie Geller Geld
Rebecca Wish Gelfand

Gary Gelfman
Sandy Gellis
Jonathan Gellman
Josh Gelman
Len Gelstein **443, 472**
Barbara Gentile
John Gentry
Cristina George
Fred George **166, 749**
Russell Gera **260**
Keith Gerchick
Dana Gerhards
Kevin Gerien
Linda Gerlach
Valery German
Hillary Geronemus
Elle Gerstler
Alfred Gescheidt
Robert Gevert
Valerie Ghent
David Giammetta
Mary Teresa Giancoli
Jennifer Gibbons
Phyllis Giber
Bruce Gilden **112, 120**
Julia Gillard **68, 69**
Kathleen Gillespie **251, 253**
Mark Gilliland
Cathleen Gillingham
James Gillson
Mark Gilman
Tim Gilmore
Erika Gimbel
Jennifer J. Gin
Micheline Gingras
David Ginsburg
Susan Ginsburg
Laurie Gioia
Dave Giordano
Kristen Girard
Lisa Giunta
David Glackin
Christopher Glasier

Kathy Glasser
Tania Glatzer
Ron Glaze
Steven Glazman
Linda Gleit
Mike Glenn
Heather Glick
Carolyn Glickstein
Beaird Glover
Michael Glowik
Billy Glucroft
Kevin Goggin **449**
Bruce Goh
William Goh
Beryl Goldberg
Nicolas Goldberg **21**
Wendy Goldberg
David Goldemberg
Anders Goldfarb
Jeffrey Goldman
Stephanie Goldman
Nancy Goldring
Joan Goldsmith
Silvianna Goldsmith
Stuart Goldstein
Jamesan Gong
June Gonzales
Brenda Gonzalez
Daniel Gonzalez
Rena Goodfriend-Leve
Cindy Goodison
Carrie Goodman
Jason Goodman
Rosabel Goodman-Everard
Doug Goodstein
Carter Goodwin
Page Goolrick
Nick Goranitis
Richard Gordon
Anthony Gordon
Richard Gordon
Spencer Gordon
Wendy Gordon **111, 175**

Alexander Gorlin
Jennifer Gorman
Michael J. Gorman **700**
Frederique Gormand
Daniel Gorrin
Arlene Gottfried
Michael Goudy
Jason Gould
Jacqueline Gourevitch
Gina Grad **600**
Monika Graff **769**
Ran Graff
Barbara Grajewski **582**
Jennifer Graley
Tracy Granger
Aidan Grant
Carol Grasso
Grace Graupe-Pillard **654**
Edward Grazda
Geoff Green
Joel Greenberg
Philip Greenberg
Marc Greendorfer
Jennifer Greene **608**
Linda Greene
Richard Greene
David S. Greenfield
Pamela Griffiths **134**
Steven Grillo
Robert Grimm
Kari Grimsby
Lori Grinker **282, 442, 674, 675**
Jane Grodenchik
Alexander Groh
Joe Groom
Alba Gross
Jeff Gross
Susan Grosse **14b, 15**
Paul Grossman **133**
Kari Grota
Nadja Groux
John Jonas Gruen **88**
Anna Gualda

Frank Schwere **584, 585, 586, 587**	Lisa Shaw	Joanne Singer	Glenn Sotzky	George Stiros **693**	K. A. Taipale	Cynthia Moran Timms **444**
Marian Schwindeman	Rachel Shaw **56, 62, 63, 78**	Marcia Singer	Andre Souroujon	Tone Stockenstrom	Miki Takada	Erik Tischler **124**
Anthony Scibilia	Beowulf Sheehan	Shirley Singer	Marcal Souto	Robert Stolarik **228, 281, 322, 323**	Ramin Talaie **678**	Susan Titsworth
Charles Scisci	Jason Sheldon **256, 263**	Jonathan Siskin	Steven Spallina	Andree Stolte	Hakim Talbi	Alex Tocaciu
Edward Scott	Barbara S. Shelley	Clifford Skeete	Tracy Spears	Erik Stone	Mario Tama **353, 359, 627, 762**	Arthur Todman
Michael Scott	Simon Sheppard	Christa Skinner	Jerry Speier	Kazuko Stone	Maria Tan	Camille Tokerud
Norris Scott	Heather Sherman	Linda Skoog	William Burks Spencer	Marilyn Stoner	Stephen Tang	Sharon Toll
Teresa S. Scripture	Zory Sherman	Peter Slack **16**	Marc Alan Sperber	Victoria Stong	Brian Tang **577**	Margaret Tomanelli **702**
Paula Alya Scully **53**	Keith Sherwood	Henry Slattery	Tom Sperduto **406, 738, 739**	Kerry Stowell	Stan Tankursley	Takaya Tomose
Stefanie Sdanowich **351**	Sheila Shettle	Tom Slaughter	Lorraine M. Spina	Frank Strangeman	Ken Tannenbaum	Betty Tompkins
Mary Anne Nash Sebby	Jody Shields	Sterne Slaven	Bill Spira	Margaret Stratton **160, 161, 163, 171**	Fred R. Tannery	Karen Tompkins
David Seccombe	Joseph Shineberg	Nancy Sloan	Daniel Springston	Carrie Strauch	Jo Ann Tansman	Nancy Tongue
Ruthanne Seconda	Jeffrey A. Shore	Spencer Sloan	Umberto Squarcia Jr.	Vera Streeter	Michael Tapes **727, 731**	Tracey Tooker
Robert Segal	Ray Short	Dave Slurzberg	Jeremy St. John Brown	Leah Streetman **13**	Geri Tapling	Maciej Toporowicz
Ann Segan	Jessie Shrieves	Lisa Small	Anthony Stamolis	Kristina Strobel	Stephen Tarter	Jonathan Torgovnik **265, 347, 565**
Lilly Sehgal	Geralyn Shukut	Maxeen Smarl	Christpher Stanley	Jeanne Strole	Bart Tarulli	JP Torres
Amy Seibert **242**	Michael Shulan/Unknown **28**	Bruce Smith	Shannon Stapleton **327**	Bruce Strong	William J. Tauchen	David Toth
Harvey Seizer	Dustin Shuler	Carter B. Smith	Ben Starkman	Carrie Struch **536**	Joseph R. Tavitas	Larry Towell **42, 47, 48, 49**
Saeko Seki	Jack Shurman	Christopher Smith **757**	Edward Stasic	Corey Struller **642**	John Bigelow Taylor	Fred Townes
Maki Sekine	Nan Shutsharawan	Jennifer Smith **640**	Martin Staudigl	Michael Strunka	Ashley Teague	Elizabeth M. Towson
Mark Seliger **85, 96, 130, 131**	Valerie Sicignano	Marion Duckworth Smith	Terry Steckowich	Gabrielle Stubbert **125, 289**	David Teeter	Stan Tracy
Helene Seligman	Jim Sicile	Maureen Smith	Alan Steele	Hal Stucker	Violet Teh	Patricia H. Trainor
Sharon L. Selwyn	Richard Siegel	Ryan & Evan Smith	Jana Stefanciosa	Johan Stylander **77**	Debbie Teicholz	Quyen Tran **553**
Cuneyt Sengul	Jeff Siegel	Sarah M.F. Smith	Jerry Stein	Carol Suchy	Mary Temple	Tuyet A. N. Tran
Russ Senzatimore	Nancy Siesel	Sharon Smith **614**	Amy Stein	Bennett M. Sugerman	John Tencza	Charles Traub **550, 551, 842**
John Senzer **844, 845**	Gerrit Sievert **488, 489**	Howard Smith Jr.	Harvey Stein	Aaron M. Sugiura	Irvin Tepper	Philip Traugott
Andrew Serban	Scott Siken	Christy Smith-Sloman	Miriam A. Stein	Patrick Sullivan **818, 819**	G. Patrick Teran	Ana Traversa
Ruth Sergel	Susan Silas	Scott Snizek	Robert Stein	Richard Sullivan **778, 792**	Keith Terracino	Viviane Travin
Chris Sergio	Lauren Silberman **610**	Alli Royce Soble	Catherine Steinmann	Dierdre Summerbell	Jim Terrell	Marie Triller
Ira Serkes	Jennifer Silva **602**	Ada B. Soby	Michael P. Stenson	Brian Sumner	Jorge Thacker **189**	Raymond Trillo
Grant Shaffer **694, 716**	Wanderlan P. Silva	Sharon Socol **755**	Ron Sterling **328**	Josh Suniewick	Barbara S. Thomas	Erik R. Trinidad
David Shaman	Darrell Silver	A. Solimene	Doug Stern	Fernanda M. Suplicy	James Thomas **238**	Leslie Trippy
Gina Shamus **759**	Scott Silverman	Caryn Solly	Burt L. Stern	David Surowiecki **232-233**	Alison Thompson **704a**	Paola Trizio **813**
Craig Shapiro	Jeffrey Silverthorne **91, 146, 147**	Keren Solomon **90**	Doug Stern	Gil Sussman	Beverly Thompson	Linda Troeller **808**
Gloria Shapiro	Laurie Simmons **564**	Robert Solywoda	Joel Sternfeld **580**	John Sutera	Karla Thompson	April Troiani
Jada Shapiro	Gabriella Simon	Judy Somerville	John Sterr	Scott Sutton	Warren K. Thompson	Michele Trombley
Michael Shapiro	Peter Angelo Simon	Chuck Sommers	Giardino Steven	Narisa Svetvilas	Alice S. Thomson	Craig Trongeau
Jeannie Sharkey	Samuel Richard Simon	Eve Sonneman	Marilyn Stevenson	Robert Swanson **615**	Juhu Thukral	Ronald Trotter
Bill Sharp **502, 503, 574**	Steve Simon **712, 713, 718, 728a, 728b**	Heidi E. Sonntag	Holly D. Stewart	Benjamin C. Swett	Charles Tibble	Danielle Troy
Brad Sharp	Gianluca Simoni **364**	Kim Sonsky	Jack Stewart	Sandra Swieder	Judy Sidonie Tillinger **243**	Michael Trueblood **276**
Katherine Baird Sharp	Joel Simpson	Christopher Soria	Melissa Stewart	Zbighiew Szachowicz	Denton Tillman **452**	Jeanny Tsai **212, 698**
Alyson Shatsky **562**	Donald Simpson Jr.	Jose Sosa	Flavio L. Stigliano	Phebe W. Szatmari	Morony Tim	Carson Tsang **264**
Robin M. Shaud	Lisa Sinatra	Tim Soter **191**	Allen Stillman	Mark Tabashnick	Millie Timmons	Linda Tseng

August C. Tsicouris
Toyo Tsuchiya
Gregory Tuck **218**
Mindy Tucker
John Tuer
Erika Tullberg
David Turnley **254, 315, 329, 376, 379, 609**
Peter Turnley **345, 409, 413, 708, 794, 795**
Tamara Turse
Mark Tusk
Joelle Tutela
Susan Tyler Jenkins
Donna M. Uher
Erica Uhlenbeck
Lydia Uhlir
Joan Ulbrich
Stephanie Umeda
Unknown Photographer **185**
Lesley Unruh **19**
Ida Unsgaard
Susan Urban
Charles Urich
Emily Urquhart
Idil Ustun
Andrea Vaaler
Matt Vacca
Matt Valentine **407**
Theresa Valla
Hector Vallenilla
Julie Van Dore
Maralyn Van Metre
Scott Van Patten
Rob Van Petten
Dennis Van Tine **451, 670**
Hanneke Van Velzen **579**
Gary Vander Patten
Michiel Vanderwal
Winston Vargas **807**
Yolanda Vasquez

Greg Veeser
David Vega
Rob Veksler
Eliot Velazquez
James Verrier
Michael Vezza
Ekasit Kaz Vichitlakakarn
Nelda Vidal
Louis Viel
Briana Viele
Cibele Viera
Peter Vietro-Hannum
Frederic Vigneron
Christopher Villano
Tanya Villanueva
Omar Villegas
Anna Vincent
Rachel Shana Vine
James Vines
Anatole Vishon
Grazia Vita
Michael Vitti
Lothar Voeller
Teun Voeten
Conrad Vogel
David Vogler
Nancy Volkman
Enzo Vollmer **639**
Mark Von Holden
Cynthia Vos-Wein
Steve Wada
Jelle Wagenaar
Beth Wagner
Sacha Waldman **620-621**
William Walicki
Alicia Walker
Andrew H. Walker
Mark Walker
Tom Walker **190**
Christopher Wall
Shona Wall

Dave Wallin-Eddy
Frank B. Walsh
Tenney Whedon Walsh
William K. Wan
Jan Wandrag
Jenny Warburg
Jenna Ward
Jesse Ward
Ira Warheit
Bernard Warkentin
Dona Warner
Elizabeth Warner
David M Warren
Kenneth Washton
Jill Waterman
George H. Waterman III
Justin Watrel
Craig Wats
Jim Watson
Teresa Watson
Elizabeth Watts
Hue Way
Alex Webb **194, 195, 310, 314**
Matt Weber
Nancy Wechter
Maureen Weicher
Tom Weigand
Stephen G. Weil
Louise Weinberg **81, 86**
Hal Weiner
Mitch Weingard
Mike Weingartner **593**
Tom Weinrich
Emily Weinstein
Lindsay Weinstein
Todd Weinstein **721**
Jack Weisberg
Katie Weisberger **862-863**
Irwin Weiss
Marty Weiss **176**
Ken Weissblum

Rebecca Weissman
James Weitzman
David Weller **532**
Howard Weller
Chris Welles
Jonathon Wells
Amy Wentz
James Wentzy **457**
Christopher M. Wertz
Lee E. Wexler **714, 715**
James Wheeldon **239**
Anthony Whitaker
Jonathan White
Pete White
Marie Whitehead
Susan Wides **634, 635**
Anthony Wieliczko
Karlene Wiese
Nancy Wight
Erin Wile
Meredith Wiley
Steve Wiley
Carey L. Wilhelm
Frank Wilk
Jeanne Wilkinson
Rebecca Wilkowski **806**
Alfred Will **305**
Inge Willers
Amani Willett
Owen Williams
W. Garrison Williams
Lauren Willner
Marjorie Wilner
Bruce Wilson
Catherine Wilson
James R. Wilson
Rosalie Winard
Jifat Windmiller
Chris Withers
Michael Witlin
Patrick Witty

Andrew Wolfson
Jill Woller
Karen Kenny Woodruff
Adam Woodward **340, 341**
Tracy Woodworth
Gregg Woolard
Joseph Woolhead
Marcus Woollen
Gene Woolridge
Sher Wouters **685**
Megan Wrenn **196**
Colin Wright
Mandi Wright
Melvin Wright **652**
Maggie Wrigley
Tony Wurman **441**
Kathleen Wyatt
Susan Wynne
Xax Xax
Norihito Yagi
Deanna Yalowitz
Shahar Yannay
Yehuda Yarimi
Richard Yasick
Christopher Yasiejko **811**
Jay Yates
Marilynn Yee
Josephine Yeh
Richard Yeh
Timur Yevtuhov
Erin Yokel **653**
Kazuhiro Yokozeki
Andrew Yonda
Yoshi **279, 434**
Miyuki Yoshihara
Jenna Yost
M. Jane Yost
Daniel Young
Lisa Young
Mary Young
Sally Young

Mark Youngberg **558**
Cheryl Younger
Seldon Shi Chi Yuan
Soo-Hwa Yuan **696**
Evan Yurman **317**
Barbara Zaffron
Bilal Zaidi
Jaroslaw Zajac **657**
Venus Zarris
Yolanta Zawada
Shirley Zeiberg
Yehuda Zeiri
Ruben Zendejas
Deborah Suchman Zeolla
Harry Zernike **343, 348, 349**
Stephanie Zessos
Dvora Zierer
Lloyd Ziff
D.A. Zimmerman
Douglas Zimmerman
Leon Zinder
Susan F. Zinder
Dan Ziskie
Charlyn Zlotnik **689**
Matt Zuckerman **114**
Stuart Zuckerman
Susie Zulich
James E. Zunt
Lisa Zwerling **699**

Every photographer who contributed a photograph to *here is new york* is equally important. If we have omitted anyone, or have misspelled anyone's name, we apologize.

volunteers

Laurence Abbasi	Susan Bell	Michael Cates	Caroline Dejean	Eve France	Janine Greges	Michael Ingbar
Donna Abbaticchil	Karen Bell	Jessica Cavuoto	Colleen Delaney	Gen Furukawa	Kelly Grider	Teru Iwasaki
John Abela	Scott Bellina	Chris Cawley	Monique Delatour	Amanda Frame	Laura Griffin	Ellen Jaffe
Jenny Acheson	Jill Bender	Diane Ceribelli	Marianne Delon	P.D. Fyke	Pamela Griffiths	Corinne James
Genevieve Adams	Andrew Berends	Amy Chang	Kelly Demaro	Judy Gabey	David Griffiths	Karen Jaroneski
Natalie Adams	Stephanie Berger	Michelle Cheikin	Jean DeNiro	Judy Gal	Kari Grimsby	Shan Jayakumar
Ron Agam	Randi Berger	Riki Cheung	Adrienne Deppe	Kia Gamburg	Mariana Gruener	Angela Jimenez
Ric Agndelo	Nicholas Bergery	Paul Chevalier	Seze Devres	Carole Gandolfo	Rona Gurin	Luke Joerger
Sandy Ahman	Maggie Berkvist	Jeremy Chien	Steve Diamond	Amy Ganti	Carlos Haase	Suzanne Johnson
Cristina Albino	Mark Bernal	Mike Chiodo	Alwyn Diaz	Raymond Garcia	Beth Hachtman	Tiffany Jones
Rita Alfonso	Ryan Beshara	Che' Chisholm	Anita Dickhuth	Jason Gardner	Mark Hado	Eve Josephsen
Toby Allan	Jon Birdseye	Clete Christopher	Isaac Dietz	Chirag Garg	Ninna Haflidadottir	Val Junker
David Allee	Star Birnbaum	Irene Christopher	Evelyn Dilworth	Anna Geisler	Crissie Haft	Susan Kaiser
Jayne Alpert	Richard Blackstone	Laurence Chua	Annie Dinerman	Steve Gelber	David Hall	Melinda Kanipe
Masaru Amano	Jacob Blickenstaff	Maggie Chula	Manny Dominguez	Kristin Gerard	Shuli Hallack	Dale Kaplan
Micahel Amoratis	Skip Blumberg	Ted Ciesielski	Elizabeth Donoff	Dana Gerhards	Leslie Hamerschlag	Josh Kaprov
Anna Armstrong	Jessica Blumenthal	Jo-Lynn Cimino	Antoine Douaihy	Julie Gervurtz	Alexis Harbour	Eleni Karas
Mark Andrew	M.J. Boensch	Sandy Ciric	Beth Dubber	Aileen Ghee	Chris Hawkins	Dennis Kardon
Lois Andrews	Sandra Boer	Janet D. Clancy	Denise Duffell	Jeremy Gibson	Tracey Lynn Haynes	Vincent Kasbi
Catherine Ang	Stacy Boge	Randall Clarke	Andrew Einhorn	Chris Gilbert	Jeannie Heifetz	Simeon Kasmetski
Jocelyn Anker	Sharyn Boswell	Al Claro	Susan Elefant	Constance Gill	Alexander Heilner	Matthew Katz
Nomi Ansari	Jessica Boucher	Lindy Cohen	Lauren Elinsky	Faye Ginsburg	Katja Heinemann	Oren Katz
Ariel Apte	Michael Bowen	Ofer Cohen	Lynn Elliot	Susan Ginsburg	Lauren Helf	Ross Kauffman
Karen Arikian	Craig Braden	Adrianna Cohen	Jonathan Ende	Michael Glowik	Beatriz Hernandez	Sara Kavner
Linda Arking	Adrianna Bravo	Corinna Collins	Steven Endich	Kevin Goggin	Terry Hildebrandt	Beat Keem
Zoe Armiger	Lara Brodzinsky	Paul Constantine	Steven Endicott	David Goldenberg	Karen Hill	Kevin Kelly
Michael Armoratis	Louise Brooks	Alex Cook	Amparo Escobedo	Stuart Goldstein	Edward Hillel	Siobhan Kennedy
Anna Armstrong	Richard V. Brown	Kevin Cooley	Beth Estrada	Jameson Gong	Deb Hiller	Liz Kennick
Tina Armstrong	Edward Buerger	John Corbett	Merrily Evans	Monica Gonzalez	David Hinder	Mark Kessell
Jane Ashe	Ben Burdsall	Esteban Cordero	Allyson Fairbanks	Annabella Gonzalez	Shinpei Hiruta	Paula Kessler
Helena Ashton	Sue Burdsall	Carol Costello	Catherine Farrel	Leah Goodman	Elise Ho	Jason Kessler
Jeannie Assogba	Jessica Burstein	Anatasia Courtney	Tara Fehner	Carter Goodwin	Kris Hochster	Sanam Khamneipur
Martha Babcock	Kate Burton	Frances Craig	Jennifer Feil	Shelley Gopal	Susan Hodes	Ronnie Kimar
Alice Baldwin	Naomi Bushman	Cynthia Crane	Neil Feiner	Wendy Gordon	Paul Hodge	William King
Iowaka Barber	Santiago Bustamante	Frank Craven	Abigail Feldman	Anthony Gordon	Moira Hodgson	Ruth Klein
Tina Barney	Jennifer Butensley	Allyson Crilly	Dawn Fenn	Linor Goren	Sydney Holly	Tom Klem
Victoria Barr	Diana Byer	Arin Crumley	Kerin Ferallo	Karla Gostnell	Stephanie Hollyman	Stacey Kmetyk
Jim Barrett	Bill Byrne	Gina Cruz	Joanne Fernando	Rachel Gould	Gillie Holme	Carol Kner
Amy Baxt	Larry Cameola	Leigh Crystal	Julie Fevola	Laney Gradus	Uli Holz	Sarah Knowlton
Priscilla Bayley	Patrick Canavan	Jed Crystal	Wendy Finkelstein	Chuck Granuille	Sujin Hong	Debra Koncan
Siham Bazzy	Patti Capaldi	Joyce Culver	Shannon Flam	Ailbhe Greaney	Ellen Horan	Carolyn Koschnick
Erica Becker	Joanne Capestro	Lucy Culver	Carol Fogel	Geoff Green	Masami Horiguchi	Adam Kowalski
Julie Becker	Al Carlo, Jr.	Kendra Cunningham	Ahron Foster	Jessica Greenbaum	Laura Horowitz	Barbara Kramer
Erica Belker	Becky Carpenter	John F. Davis	Ken Foster	Allyson Greene	Kim Hubbard	Dick Kramer
Adam Bell	Claudia Carr	Nick DeCresce	Jimmy Fountain	Terrence Greene	Lyn Hughes	Douglas Krugman
Alastair Bell	Marlen Casanova	Paul Degeorge	Amy Fox	Sally Greenspan	Katherine Hung	Melissa Krupanski

Kaja Kuhl	John Mazlish	Marguerite Oerlemans	Lisa Rayman	Jaime Schlesinger	Lianna Sugarman	Ira Warheit
Susan Kuhlman	Florence Mazzone	Kiyomi Okubo	Juan Recaman	Carol Schlitt	Josh Suniewick	Tom Warren
Barbara Kurgan	Christine McAndrews	Adria Olender	Arianne Recto	Tom Schmitt	Barbara Suomi	Rebecca Norris Webb
Monica Lamontagne	Suzanne McConnell	Jennifer Olive	Piotr Redlinski	Beth Schneckenburger	Fernanda Matarazzo Suplicy	Amy Webster
Mischa Lampert	Molly McGarry	Petra Olton	Andrea Star Reese	Sonia Schoenholtz	Ayako Suzuki	Tracy Webster
Kelli Langley	Stacy McGoldrick	Heather Oppelt	Beverly Reese	Lisa Schorr	Sandra Swieder	Maureen Weicher
John Larocca	Katy McLaughlin	Suzanne Opton	Star Reese	Laura Schwamb	Mario Tama	Shelley Weinstock
Catherine Lascoumes-	Caroline McNamara	Attilla Ozdemir	Roy Reid	Arlene Schwartz	Gloria Tanner	Melody Weir
Friedman	Nina McNamara	Anita Pagliaro	Dorothy A. Reilly	Deborah Schwartz	Ricardo Tarrega	Katie Weisberger
Johanna Latty	Amy-Beth McNeely	Paulette Palami	Lorie Rein	Ross Schwartzman	John Taylor	Bob Weiss
Dana Lavi	Lara McPherson	Hila Paldi	Lori Reinstein	Jocelyn See	Jennifer Taylor	Rebecca Weissman
Cindy Lawrence	Rose Anne Mendes	Marcy Palmer	Andrea Retzy	Christian Seikmeier	Ashley Teague	Nikki Wella
Roz Lechter	Victoria Miano	Stefano Paltera	Lou Ricchio	Dena Seki	Robin Telerant	David Weller
Benjamin Lee	Rachel Milano	Suellen Parker	Deborah Rivers	Ken Semeraro	Drew Thomas	Amy Wentz
Rebecca Leicht	Andrea Milo	Mitchell Parnes	Marilena Rizzo	Ruth Sergel	Tanya Thomas	Randy West
Carlos Lema	Lisa Minicino	Craig Paulson	Elisabeth Robert	Chris Sergio	Daysie Tiu	Meredith White
Regina H. Leonard	Michael Pazy Mino	Justin Pauly	Abby Robinson	Carlo Shaase	Leonard Todd	Sally Wigutow
Barbara Lettman	Carmenza Minotta	Robert Peacock	Shaunti Rocher	Annie Shapiro	Jackie Tolkowsky	Rick Wijensbeek
Neil Leventhal	Zoe Moffitt	Alice B. Pearce	Cecilia Rodhe	Dana Shapiro	Nancy Tongue	Lesley Williams
Meg Levine	Justine Mojica	Lisa Pete	Rod Rodriguez	Jack Sherman	Leshu Torchin	Suzanne Williamson
Steve Levine	Juan Molinari	Marie-Louise Petitpierre	Dorian Romer	Meiko Shibata	Chris Toward	Catherine Wilson
Susan Levit	Livia Monaco	Chris Picco	Lauren Ronick	Shelly Shicoff	Christine Tracey	Jifat Windmiller
Mary Liao	Bill Morel	Tara Pietz	Jose Rosario	Dwayne Shirley	Jud Traphagen	Gayle Wingo
Rosalind Lichter	Michelle Morelli	Anna Pinto	Ivy Rosen	Kathy Shorr	Aaron Traub	Ofer Wolberger
Eliane Lingwood	Tricia Morente	Sebastian Piras	Lynn Rosensweig	Alexander Shulan	Mary Traub	Jeroen Woltman
Jonathon Lipkin	Ricki Moskowitz	Rajal Pitroda	Mimi Roterman	Rachel Shuman	Terry Treanor	Cheryl Wong
Andrew Loevenguth	Rachel Movitz	Lisa Pitz	Lawrence Royer	Nan Shutsharawan	Patti Treger	Adam Woodward
Paul Lombardi	Laura Mozes	Vicky Pizzino	Laura Rubin	Joan Gottlieb Siegel	Rob Trenchard	Yuki Yamaguchi
Melissa Longo	Steven Mudrick	Niko Plaitakis	Irma Rusk	Jill Sigman	Moe Tribelsi	Jossephine Yeh
Mark Lubell	Edwin Mullon	Jonathan Podwil	Sharon Rutter	Teresa Signarelli	Miyuki Tsushima	Angela Yoo
Susan Luciano	Blerti Murataj	Judy Polzer	Jeff Rutzky	Lauren Silbeman	Marguerite Tully	Bilal Zaidi
Chi Tien Lui	John Murphy	Miriam Poser	Yael Daphna Saar	Karolyn Silver	Debbie Ullman	Deanna Zandt
Allen Maertz	Sam Myers	Amanda Powers	Tamera Sakovska	Katherine Silverblatt	Daniel Valdez	Yolanta Zawada
Tim Main	Reggie Nadelson	Joanna Pressman	Miriam Salholz	Joanne Sirgado	Kathy Valko	Stephanie Zessos
Lisa Maizush	Charlotte Ng	Carolyn Protass	Amy Saltz	Christa Skinner	Julia Van Haaften	Jade Zhou
Salome Makharadze	Vince Navarro	Ron Purdy	Gulnara Samoilova	Sara Slater	Peggy Vanderpool	Susan Ziluca
Carolyn Mandt	Bruno Navarro	Rina Rachman	Jason Samuels	Kristina Snyder	Jessie Vanderveen	Sally Zunino
Brenda English Manes	Lara Nebel	Greg Rachwalski	Catalino Santamaria.	Sharon Gurman Socol	Nikki Vilella	Erica Zurer
Paul Manes	Pam Nesbitt	Peter Rad	Luisa Santos	Linda Solodar	David Vogler	
Jay Manis	Laurie Neustadt	Sharon Rader	Sarah Sapora	Maxine Spencer	Jordan Volan	
Anna Manuel	Carole Newhouse	Susan Rae	Ken Sato	Pat Spitalieri	Penne Vose	
Dona Marans	Paige Newman	Marcee Raffel	Rich Scarpitta	Cory Stebel	Kelly Waldron	
Kathryn Martell	Brian Noalhn	Rachel Randolph	Scott Schedivy	Stephanie Stegich	Sarina Wallack	
Nadja Masri	Susan Nolgren	Alexis Raskin	Stephanie Schenppe	Jade Stice	Ellen Wallenstein	
Lili Matsuda	Beth O'Donnell	Linda Raskin	Nancy Scherl	Ginny Stillman	Tenney Walsh	
Claudia Mattiello	John O'Sullivan	Dave Rauch	Lisa Schlahet	David Strom	Jenna Ward	

We are profoundly indebted to every volunteer who joined us at *here is new york*. If anyone has been omitted, or has been listed incorrectly, we apologize.

try this at home

All of the photographs in this book were originally printed with inexpensive inkjet printers, as were the majority of the tens of thousands of prints which we have printed and sold for charity. We have continued to use these printers because we find the prints they produce to be distinctive, and distinctively beautiful. They are very different from glossy commercial prints or shiny photos in magazines. Their matte texture and colors are not dull but rich, with great depth and tonal range. They look, at once, unmistakably photographic and yet not quite like any other photographs that we have seen before.

That being said, there is another almost equally important reason why we continue to use this equipment. We firmly believe in the power of inexpensive and uncomplicated technology. Although operating these printers on a large scale has not exactly been easy for us—for much of the past year we have had dozens of them running twenty-four hours a day (and burning out, it should be noted, every few weeks), *here is new york* could not have come into being without them. Back when there were only a few of us operating with borrowed and scavenged equipment, they were our only option. The fact that they are as good as they are, and as simple to operate, played no small part in our story.

Printing as we do is something within the reach of almost any photographer. All it requires are digital images, a modest computer, and a good inkjet printer. Printers of this sort are available from a variety of manufacturers and are improving all the time, even as they become more and more affordable. Here are some general guidelines:

• Everything begins with the digital file. Images donated to *here is new york* have come in virtually every form: traditional negatives, slides, prints, and files from digital cameras. When scanning, larger files are not only better, they are critical. For this book's reproductions, and for our prints, scans from prints and negatives have been saved as *tiff* files (LZW lossless compression) at no less than 150 ppi:

300 ppi or more is even better. Our 24-bit color files average 20–40 mb; our 8-bit black-and-white files, 12–15 mb. (Note: it is always better to scan not from the print but from the film, whether it is a negative or a slide.)

• Many of our pictures have been taken with digital cameras, which range widely in quality and maximum file size. Again, the bigger the file, the better (or larger) the print can be. In order to print large images from digital camera files, the camera should be set to record the fewest possible number of pictures. Most consumer cameras record their images as jpegs, which, although much smaller than optimum tiffs, can give extremely good results. Set the camera to use the least amount of compression possible.

• After conversion to electronic files, check your images for dust and scratches and color correct them for your printer, a process that will depend upon your images and particular equipment. We do this work with Adobe Photoshop. Save your color images in the Image> Mode> Assign profile of Adobe (1998) RGB (for Macintosh or Windows). Save your black-and-white images in the Image> Mode> Assign profile of Gray Gamma 1.8 (for Macintosh), and Gray Gamma 2.2 (for Windows).

• We print everything on A3 paper, which is approximately 16.5 by 11.7 inches. When using matte heavyweight paper, which is what we prefer, set your printer to 720 dpi, even if will print at higher resolution, since matte paper is quite absorbent and too much ink will tend to muddy the image. For glossy paper, you will need to print at 1440 dpi to get good results.

As with anything, it will take some practice and experimentation to get things right. But the technology involved is not really very complicated, and is getting simpler and better all the time.

For more information, consult our website: www.hereisnewyork.org.

friends and patrons

A. P. Tobin Construction
Aaron Siskind Foundation
Ace Audio Visual
Vince Aletti
Toni Allocca
American Express
Andy Warhol Foundation
Apple Computer, Inc
Appleman Foundation
Michael Armstrong
Ken Aso
Astor Liquors
George Audisio
Rémi Babinet
Caroline Banker
Banque CCF
Tina Barney
Adam Behar
Alastair Bell
Patrick Benasillo
Jacqueline Bennett, Esq.
Melissa Bent
BETC EURO RSCG
Jean-Pierre Biron
Victoria Bjorklund, Esq.
Philip Block
Brooklyn Brewery
Philip Brookman
Debra Burke
Ken Burkhardt
Craig Buthod
Canteen Restaurant
Dawn Carmilia
James Carrecker
Catch Light Productions
CAVS Ltd.
Chasanoff Foundation
Chicago Department of Cultural Affairs
Chicago Hilton Towers
Jeremy Chien
Children's Aid Society
David Chipkin
Citibank
Philip Coltoff
Columbia College of Chicago
Condé Nast
Cookes Catering
Richard A. Corbett
The Corcoran Gallery of Art

CorporArt Communication
Juan Corradi
Charles de Croisset
Eric Tong Cuong
CyberSource
Davis and Grutman, LLP
Pierre Decasanove
Maria Delgado
Felix Dennis
Adrianne Deppe
Diogenes Charitable Foundation
Milton DiPietro
DPI, Inc.
Dublin Fire Brigade
Luke Dudd
Durst Organization
Charles Duval
Ecrix Corporation
Adam Eisenstat
EM Consulting, LLC
Epson Corporation
Mercedes Erra
Harold M. Evans
Joseph Farrelly
Nathan Felde
Sandi Fellman
FEMA
Michael Finneran
Susan E. Fischer
Josh Fisher
Ellen Fleurov
Flow Lounge
Fotocare, Inc.
Amanda Frame
Linda Frankel
Virginia Friedlaender
Jim Friestad
Linda Fritzinger
Tomoyasu Fukunaga
Peter Galassi
Philip Gefter
Getty Images
Howard Greenberg
Howard Grubner
Bennet Grutman
GSM, Inc.
Nick Hartman
Willis Hartshorn
Joyce Healy

Donald Healy
Francois Hebel
Moira Hodgson
Vinod Hopson
Horace W. Goldsmith Foundation
Howard and Sharon Socol
    Family Foundation
Howard Greenberg Gallery
Hulton/Archive
Imacon
Michael Ingbar
International Center of Photography
Jarvis Irving & Co. LLP
ISIS Films
J. R. Display
Jarvis Irving Company, LLP
JGS Foundation
Liz Jobey
Chuck Jones
Zella Jones
Val Junker
Bill Katz
Bicky Kelner
Mark Kessell
Kingsfountain
Virginia Kinsey
Jonathan Klein
Eastman Kodak Co.
Thomas Krueger
Rosalind Lichter, Esq.
Susan Luciano
John Macintosh
Tim Main
Manhattan Beer Distributors
Jonathan Marder
Karen Marta
Kay Lowe Masuhr
Jun Matsui
Angie Mattos
George McPherson
Harry McPherson
Luisella Meloni
Ronay Menschel
Michael Ingbar Gallery
Mimi Ferzt Gallery
Susan Modenstein
Edwin Mullon
Arne Mutert
Chantal Nedjib

New York Cares
New York Times
Jacob Newfelt
Doerte Nimz
Nino's Restaurant
Susan Nolgren
Virginia O'Grady
Patte O'Reilly
Olive's Restaurant
116 Prince Street, LLC
Mark Oster
Alfred Pacquement
Panasonic
Panix
Paraskevas Gallery
Paxton Companies
Jacob Peck
Susan Penzner
Danny Pepper
Pete's Place
Pete's Restaurent
Peter S. Reed Foundation
Ben Pfeffer
Henry Pillsbury
Amy Sloan Pinel
Joanna Pressman, Esq.
Prince Street Copy
Professional Graphics, Inc.
Project We Care
Qualex, an Eastman Kodak Company
Richard Rabinowitz
Peter Rad
Carmen Ramos
Reel 3-D Enterprises, Inc.
Bruno Reichert
John Reynolds
David Rhodes
Anthony Rhodes
David Rhodes
Silas Rhodes
Susanne Rockweiler
Paul Roth
Jan Rothschild
Royal and Son Alliance Insurance
Ruder Finn, Inc.
Masumi (Saki) Sakikawa
Miranda Salt
Susan Sarandon
Etienne Sauret

Herbert Schiffrin
Allon Schoener
Nathan Schoener
School of Visual Arts
Ivan Schwartz
Scitex Corporation Ltd.
Jacquelin Serwer
Robert Shapiro
Shiseido Cosmetics (America), Ltd.
Kathy Shorr
Marissa Shorr
Maggie Simmons
Simpson, Thacher Bartlett
Thomas Slaughter
Charles Smith
Justin Smith
Roberta Smith
Norma Smurfit
Sharon Grurman Socal
Social Teez
Christine Sperber
Spy Bar
Barbara Stefany
Jack Stefany
Howard Stein
Jan Stein
Dan Steinhardt
Cindy Stivers
Jeffrey Studley
Target Corporation
Louise Tarolan
Steve Tarter
Tarter Stats Realty
Tekserve
Masaru Tersaki
Iwasaki Teru
Fred Towns
Tranquil Money
Sonia Travers
Marguerite Tully
Joseph Tuohy
Susan Unterberg
Urban Academy
Gary Van Dis
Verio, Inc.
Viewpoint Corporation
Visual Graphic Systems, Inc.
Diane von Furstenberg
Serena Wallach

Syuichi Watanabe
Wendy Watriss
Barbara Watson
Randy West
Westin Hotel Dublin
Robert Williams
James Wintner
Jean-Philippe Witwicki
Paul Wombell
Wood Printcraft
Woodford Bourne, Ltd.
Masahiko Yamamoto
Vivian El Yashar
Diana Zentay
John Zentay
Alice Zimet
Zones, Inc.

Whether or not they have
been listed here by name,
here is new york is extremely
grateful to the thousands of
individuals and entities who
have supported us.

here is new york would like
to thank the following
agencies and organizations
for photographs which are
included in this book.

The Associated Press
Aurora & Quanta Productions
Contact Press Images
Corbis
Corbis Saba
FEMA
Gamma Press
Getty Images
London Features International
Magnum Photos
The Newark Star-Ledger
Reuters
Sipa Press

here is new york:

a project by Alice Rose George – Gilles Peress – Michael Shulan – Charles Traub

book credits:

designed by Yolanda Cuomo and Gilles Peress

edited by Alice Rose George and Gilles Peress

text by Michael Shulan

project management by Charles Traub

produced by Chris Boot

design associate, Kristi Norgaard

digital production:
Paul Constantine
Abigail Feldman
Kevin Goggin
Brenda English Manes
Lara McPherson
with
Masaru Amano
Santiago Bustamante
Jed Crystal
Seze Devres
Kari Grimsby
Oren Katz
Carlos Lema
Deb Schwartz
Ross Schwartzman
Miyuki Tsushima

editorial research:
Suzanne Williamson
with
Martha K. Babcock
Maggie Berkvist
Lucy Culver
Jay Manis
Debbie Ullman

printed by Dr. Cantz'sche Druckerei, Germany

www.hereisnewyork.org

© 2002 by here is new york, inc., a 501 (c)(3) not-for-profit corporation

the photographs in this book © 2002 by the photographers (see list)

this edition © 2002 by Scalo Zurich - Berlin - New York
Head office: Weinbergstrasse 22a, CH-8001 Zurich/Switzerland,
phone: 41 1 261 0910, fax: 41 1 261 9262,
e-mail: publishers@scalo.com, website: www.scalo.com

http://www.scalo.com/ All rights reserved. No part of this book may be reproduced
or utilized in any form or by any means, electronic or mechanical including photocopying,
recording, or by information storage and retrieval system, without the written
permission in writing from the publishers or here is new york, inc.

Distributed in North America by D.A.P./Distributed Art Publishers, Inc., NY, NY;
in Europe, Africa, and Asia by Thames and Hudson, London;
in Germany, Austria, and Switzerland by Scalo.

Second Scalo Edition 2002
ISBN 3-908247-66-7
Printed in Germany

**this edition made possible through the generous support of
the Volkart Foundation, Winterthur/Switzerland**